WE KEPT THE SECRET
NOW IT CAN BE TOLD

WE KEPT THE SECRET
NOW IT CAN BE TOLD

Some Memories

of Pembroke V Wrens

Collected

&

Edited by

Gwendoline Page

Dedicated to all the
Members of the W.R.N.S.
who served at
Bletchley Park and outstations

Books by the same author:

'Coconuts and Coral' First published 1993
'Growing Pains – A Teenager's War' First published 1994
'They Listened in Secret – More memories of the Wrens' First published 2003
'The Chocolate Elephant' First published 2007

10 DIGIT ISBN 0-900616-65-2
13 DIGIT ISBN 978-0-900616-65-5

Printed and published by
Geo. R. Reeve Ltd., 9-11 Town Green, Wymondham, Norfolk

ACKNOWLEDGEMENTS

There is a long list of names of people I must acknowledge, for without their help this book would not have come together.

First of all I would like to mention all those ex-Wrens who wrote to me personally with their own memories of life as a Special Duties Wren. They include:

Pamela Mack	Phyllis Shore	Rita Jenner
Ann Mcnish	Anne Lewis-Smith	Kay Roe
Elspeth Clay	Sylvia Pulley	Roma Davies
Vera Lister	Merrie Acton	Audrey Wind
Peggy Erskine-Tulloch	Barbara Beach	Ruth Bourne
Beryl Martin	Diana Neale	Jenny Conduit
Doreen Clayton	Dorothy Du Boisson	Anne Finding
Cynthia Waterhouse	Enid Seagrove	Betty Brook
Louise Barrie	Rae Cross	Rosemary Lyster
Betty Mayall	Joan Unwin	Joan Dinwoodie
Daphne Child	Joan Cole	Margaret Sharman
Doris Kandler	Margaret Francis	Kay Pickett
Winifred Stokes	Bobs Brook-Taylor	Dorothy Smith
Joan Bailey	Mary Moore	
Margaret Rowe	Rosemary Podd	

I should also like to thank Margaret Henderson who had already collected some of the memories of those who worked in the Japanese section at Bletchley Park and passed them on for me to include in this book; also Catherine Caughey who gave me permission to include some extracts from her book "World Wanderer".

Anthony (Tony) E. Sale F.B.C.S. has been most helpful in providing more technical descriptions of the Turing Bombe Machine and the Colossus Decoding Machine on which many of the Wrens worked for the understanding of those readers who are more technically inclined than myself.

I should also like to say a special 'Thank You' to Sir Philip Duncombe, Past Chairman of the Bletchley Park Trust, for kindly agreeing to write a foreword to this book in answer to my letter 'from out of the blue'.

FOREWORD

by Sir Philip Duncombe Bt DL
Chairman – Bletchley Park Trust 1997-2000

I have read the manuscript of this book with admiration and fascination. I am tremendously impressed by the vivid retention of memories by so many people covering the vital period of World War II, albeit now 55 years ago.

For my part I am honoured to have been asked to write this foreword as at the time I was a 12 year old schoolboy living with my parents at Great Brickhall where I and my family live now. I remember our spare rooms being booked in 1938 "in case the Foreign Office want to use them if there's a war". The day war was declared three 'mystery' men arrived; Commander Denniston, Nigel de Grey and Colonel Jeffery. My father immediately recognised Nigel de Grey from Eton school days back in 1902 whereupon the latter explained his presence by telling us he was a Director of the Medici Gallery in London.

Sadly my father died in 1971, three years before the first book was published on Ultra, so he knew nothing about the background of the first three men who lived with us seven days a week during the first phase of the war, except that they worked at "the hush-hush place at Bletchley". Their regular supper menu was rabbit, and I used to be sent to the Post Office to collect 21 shillings each per week.

I wish every success to this exciting historical account and to all its contributors.

INTRODUCTION

By now, due to television programmes and the many books written on the subject, most people know of the part Bletchley Park, or Station X as its codename was, played in the Second World War. However, they may not know that of the twelve thousand people working there by the end of the war many were members of the Womens Royal Naval Service, usually referred to as Wrens. Wrens also helped to man the many outstations such as Eastcote, Stanmore, as well as stations overseas such as H.M.S. Anderson in Colombo, Ceylon (now Sri Lanka). Their work covered many sections in these highly secret decoding stations and all were obliged to keep their work secret for many years both during and after the war ended. It was not until the late 1970s that we were able to speak of the work we did. By that time it was too late to tell many of those who were close to us. For myself, my parents died before I could tell them, so they never knew what part I had played, small though it may have been, towards the final conclusion of hostilities.

During the last year or so I have been gathering from those remaining ex-wrens (now in their seventies and eighties) some memories of their time as a PV Wren on Special Duties. The memories cover both work and play, and generally the life we led at the time. Some stories are highly amusing, some serious and some sad. I have enjoyed reading them all and give my grateful thanks to those who dug into their memories and made the effort to write to me. I hope those who read this book will find as much pleasure and interest as I have done. The stories may surprise their grandchildren!

The following little verse was on the back of the menu card of the St. George's Day Millennium lunch held by the Norwich Branch of the Association of Wrens:

> We're recycled, reconditioned,
> And rejuvenated too.
> We all look simply perfect,
> After all that we've been through.
> Despite the passage of the years
> The fact remains still true,
> We're the greatest group of retreads
> To emerge from World War Two   *Anon*

"We were born before television, before penicillin, polio vaccine, frozen foods, photocopiers, contact lenses, videos, frisbees and the Pill. We lived before radar, credit cards, split atoms, laser beams and ball point pens; before dishwashers, tumble dryers, electric blankets, air conditioners, drip dry clothes and before man walked on the moon.

We were born before day care centres, group homes and disposable nappies. We had not heard of FM radio, tape decks, electric typewriters, artificial hearts, word processors, yogurt and men wearing earings. For us 'time sharing' meant togetherness, a chip was a piece of wood or a fried potato. Hardware meant nuts and bolts and software was not even a word.

Before 1945 "Made in Japan" meant junk. The term "making out" referred to how you did in your exams. A stud was something that fastened a collar to a shirt and "going all the way" meant staying on a double decker bus until it reached the depot.

Pizzas, MacDonalds and instant coffee were unheard of. In our day, cigarette smoking was fashionable, grass was mown, coke was kept in the coalhouse, a joint was a piece of meat you had on a Sunday and pot was something you cooked in. Rock music was a grandmother's lullaby, El Dorado was an ice cream and a gay person was the life and soul of the party".

Extracts taken from a letter written by Alan E. George to the Diamond Circle. Appropriate to those of us born before 1945. No wonder some of us can be confused!

CONTENTS

History of SDX Wrens at Bletchley Park   x

Chapter 1 – Early Days at Station X   1
Pamela Mack, Elsbeth Clay, Peggy Erskin-Tulloch,
Ann McNish, Vera Lister

Chapter 2 – Impressions of Park and Quarters   8
Beryl Martin, Cynthia Waterhouse, Betty Mayall,
Doris Kandler, Gwendoline Page, Margaret Rowe,
Anne Lewis-Smith, Doreen Clayton, Louise Barrie,
Daphne Child, Winifred Stokes, Joan Baily,
Phyllis Shore, Sylvia Pulley

Chapter 3 – Woburn Abbey   43
Catherine Caughay, Barbara Beach,
Dorothy Du Boisson, Rae Cross, Merrie Acton,
Diana Neale, Enid Seagrove, Dorothy Smith

Chapter 4 – Spies?   70
Joan Unwin, Joan Cole

Chapter 5 – The Japanese Section Hut 7   73
Margaret Henderson, Edith Becker, Bunny Borland,
Brenda Kelly, Beryl Winter, Eunice Philips, Winifred Pitt,
Doris Watson, Kay Pickett, Merrie Acton, Pam Adams,
Betty Everest, Beryl Middleton, Ruth Perry,
Margaret Picken, Joan Stevens, Belle Watson

Chapter 6 – Eastcote and Stanmore   81
Margaret Francis, Mary Moore, Rita Jenner,
Roma Davies, Ruth Bourne, Anne Finding,
Bobs Brook-Taylor, Rosemary Podd, Kay Roe,
Audrey Wind, Jenny Conduit

Chapter 7 – 'Y' Section WT and DF Operators   108
Betty Brook, Rosemary Lyster

Chapter 8 – Wrens Overseas   117
Joan Dinwoodie, Sylvia Pulley, Margaret Sharman,
Joan Russell, Ann McNish, Gwendoline Page,
Enid Seagrove

Conclusion   168

HISTORY OF SDX WRENS AT BLETCHLEY PARK

**WRNS Superintendent Blagrove based at Walton Hall wrote a
History of the Wrens at GCCS dated 6th October 1945. From
this, I have taken the following information.**

Five WRNS Officers were the first members of the Service to arrive
at Bletchley Park, appointed for a course on 15th February 1941.
One, Third Officer Ziman, returned in October 1941 to work
permanently in the establishment.

The first contingent of ratings, 1 Leading Wren and 7 Wrens
arrived on 24th March 1941, not knowing what their work would
be. They lived in billets in Bletchley which were famed for their
lack of baths. They were all known as 'Writer' category, but were
allocated to the Bombe sections, working on Alan Turing's
machines. Doubt was felt in some quarters as to whether women
could undertake the work. By February 1942 they had proved their
worth and numbers increased as they replaced men and their
category was allocated as "Special Duties X". They had gained
official recognition.

In December 1942, WRNS in Station X became known as HMS
Pembroke V. Many attempts were made to find a suitable category
badge, but security reasons made this difficult and it was considered
advisable to leave the category badgeless.

Many difficulties occurred in the early days in the struggle to
live. Ration cards failed to appear, bath and laundry situation
caused headaches, and medical and dental arrangements had to be
made. Billet problems occurred frequently.

There was magnificent spirit among these pioneers and great co-
operation and help from those around them. The stimulation was
the knowledge of the essential work on which they were employed.
Their keenness to do well and their enthusiasm was an inspiration
for all who came later. These ratings were destined to be the future
Officers and Chief Wrens of their section.

In February 1942, new entries were interviewed in Training
Depots by an officer from Station X before being accepted for the
category, and after this date there was no transfer permitted from

this category, except on medical grounds, unsuitability, or very strong compassionate reasons.

From this beginning, developed an organisation of WRNS numbering 2,963. The majority operating the machines in Bombe Section, where they were sited at Adstock, Wavendon, Gayhurst, Stanmore and Eastcote, but Wavendon was closed down and eventually became WRNS quarters. SDX ratings in this section were trained in teleprinting, and switchboard operating, thus avoiding outside categories being employed. By December 1944, 1,699 were working in this section. Naval Section employed 2 WRNS Officers and 5 ratings, but by August 1945 numbers had risen to 570 Officers and ratings. Hut 6 started with Wrens in May 1942, by May 1945 they were employing 161 Officers and ratings.

Mr. Newman's section (Colossus) was entirely staffed by WRNS personnel who worked under civilian technicians. In May 1943 there were 16 ratings; by May 1945 there was a total of 270 Officers and ratings.

After the end of the European War, Bombes, Hut 6 and many in Mr. Newman's Section became redundant.

It was decided to transfer 200 ratings to Hollerith under Mr. Freeborn and Japanese section absorbed 48. Another 8 formed a small section under Wing Commander Smith.

The first party of SDX were drafted overseas in February 1943 and from then onwards batches were sent out first to Kilindini (E. Africa) and later to HMS Anderson in Colombo, Ceylon, reaching a total of 290.

Accommodation for all WRNS personnel in Station X was found by requisitioning the following properties as WRNS Quarters:

Steeple Claydon	January 1942
Walton Hall	February 1942
Crawley Grange	March 1942
Wavendon House	May 1942
Gayhurst Manor	August 1942
Stanmore	September 1942 specially constructed
Crawley Rectory	May 1943
Woburn Abbey	July 1943
Eastcote	August 1943 specially constructed
Stockgrove Park	August 1944
Walton Rectory	December 1944
Wavendon Park Farm	February 1945

These Quarters were staffed by WRNS Cooks and Stewards under the charge of experienced Quarters Officers, responsible for the welfare of the WRNS to Senior Wrens Administrative Officer.

First Officer Canale from December 1941 to October 1942
Chief Officer MacKenzie from October 1942 to May 1944
Chief Officer Blagrove from May 1944 to February 1945 when the post was upgraded to Superintendent, in which capacity she served until September 1945, when, due to decrease in personnel, the post reverted to Chief Officer and was filled by Chief Officer Salmond.

Officers in Charge had access to Sections to enable them to co-operate with heads of Departments.

As numbers increased, liaison technical administrative officers were appointed to each section, proving invaluable from the administrative point of view and relieving heads of sections of many petty administrative queries.

During the latter part of 1943 Crawley Rectory was transferred to a Sick-Quarters with a resident medical officer and nursing staff.

In the Spring of 1945, a Mobile Dental Unit was allocated to the Bletchley area in the charge of a Dental Surgeon.

In November 1944, the civilian cafeteria was unable to continue to supply meals to Service personnel and it was decided to open a WRNS Cafeteria in the Park staffed by WRNS Officers, Cooks and Stewards. Meals were also provided for all Naval personnel, including Americans and Canadians, and at the peak served 1,000 meals a day.

Superintendent Blagrove concludes:

"Quarters are quickly closing down as WRNS become redundant to their sections and large numbers have remustered into other WRNS categories, and by 31st December 1945 the SDX Category will be obsolete".

CHAPTER 1

THE EARLY DAYS AT STATION X

From PAMELA MACK ex-3/0 WALKER

I was one of the first eight wrens to arrive at Bletchley Park Hut 11 in March 1941.

We came from Greenwich where we did our probationary training. The entire month there we never slept above ground on account of the Air Raids which were fairly intense. Then we 'sailed under sealed orders' to Euston Station where we heard that our destination was Bletchley. We were all in mufti (civilian dress) as the uniform factory had been bombed. We just had W.R.N.S. arm-bands. On arrival at Bletchley we were allocated billets in the town. By this time the best of the billets had been taken up by the Civil Servants. My partner and I were put up in a railway cottage not far from the Park. Our landladies son used to sleep in my bed when we were on night watch, ... witness grey hairs in the bed! ... Two friends of mine had to share a double bed never having met before! However, there was nowhere else to go, so we put up with it. Our social was the 'Garden Cafe' in Bletchley.

Initially Wrens were chosen to operate the Bombs (decoding machines) as an experiment, largely due to Commander Travis RN who was the head of Administration at B.P. (Bletchley Park). He favoured the Navy 'having a go'. We didn't let him down – witness 2000 odd Wren Bombe Operators by the end of the war – largely aided by RN and RAF ex GPO engineers who kept the 'mechanics' in order. I feel very strongly that they have not been recognised sufficiently.

Note. After some publicity had been given to my work at wartime Bletchley Park by the Eastern Daily Press, I received a number of letters from interested people. Among them was a letter from a Mr Peter Smith who was one of the Post Office Engineers who maintained the Typex machines operated by the Wrens who worked in Block D. The engineers workshop was in Hut 24 which housed a staff of 20, all of whom were on 24 hour duties. Others were in

1

various blocks where A.T.S. and WAAF personnel operated Typex machines. In 1945 Mr Smith was sent to Berlin where he opened communications from there to the Foreign Office in London. He handed the service over to traffic and the first official messages from there after the war were sent by Peter Halliday. Peter Halliday was awarded the O.B.E. for starting the Berlin-London transmissions, but the work had been done earlier by Peter Smith who remained in Berlin for two and a half years. (GP)

In 1942 Wren Quarters were acquired at North Crawley Grange, a definite improvement on the billets, but very remote, and for 'days off' we largely relied on 'hitch-hiking'. Some of us sent for cycles which made life more interesting. Watch-keeping was more of a problem. By this time I was CPO (Chief Petty Officer) and all four watch CPOs shared a room with two bunks, so there was always someone sleeping – or trying to! There was a bathroom at Crawley shared by forty – One night a man got in!! (Pamela does not tell us the resulting end of this story).

The trip in to B.P. by coach took 3/4 hour, which extended the eight hour watches by 1 1/2 hours, otherwise we had no means of getting out to North Crawley – I never knew there was a lake at B.P. until I went to the first reunion.

In 1943 a nucleus of us went to open up Stanmore. It was a shell of a building intended for a hospital at the end of the Edgeware Road. Initially we scrubbed it on our hands and knees! As far as our lives were concerned it was a great improvement as we could get on the underground Bakerloo line and have a day off in the West End. Each watch had its own bay for sleeping with smaller rooms off for the P.Os, and the ablutions.

In 1944 again a nucleus was hived off from Stanmore to go and start Eastcote, – a similar set up but larger. They had 200 strong watches – we had 150. There were also a number of Americans at Eastcote. We had none at Stanmore.

ANN McNISH (nee MARCEL)

After my 18th birthday in August 1940 I applied to join the W.R.N.S. After a long struggle with interviews and medical I was called up to be at the Royal Naval College, Greenwich, Queen Anne Block on the 16th June 1941. We were given all sorts of chores there including washing up in the galley and lectures on Royal

Naval ranks, etc. Lots of marching culminating in a parade for Princess Marina, who arrived by boat.

We were issued with uniform and pay book and number (16728). There were no sailor hats at that time, but hats with brims. B.P. wrens were the first to be issued with the new cap. Very soon after the new issue two of us spent three days in Edinburgh, the caps drew lots of stares!

Five of us received our draft to Bletchley. We all said "Where's that?" Superintendent Mrs Lawes allowed us to stay over for the parade and then we were off to Euston for the journey to B.P. We were put up in billets. Mine was a lodge to a farm at Haversham near Wolverton. I was horrified to find no running water, a loo down the garden and a candle to bed! The landlady was sweet and brought me a jug of hot rain water to wash in. I rang home in tears, but had no sympathy, just told to get on with it. Anne Pease by this time had joined and we got together and found digs in New Bradwell with Mr and Mrs Bunce. They had a real loo. Such joy! To get a bath we booked one at the Mansion (in the Park). What a start with that and the sight of the Bombe we were to operate. Survival was the order and a big lesson. Walton Hall was opened and we all moved in. What JOY! Real loos and baths.

I was sitting in the common room one day doing my needlework when who walked in with the Quarters Officer but the Director of WRNS Mrs Laughton Matthews. She showed a lot of interest in conditions at Walton and asked many questions, such as was there anything we needed? I suggested an iron and board would be useful. We got it. She was very caring of 'her Wrens' and a delight to talk to.

At B.P. Anne Zeppinger and Sgt. Jones instructed us on operating the Bombes. When I arrived, there were three in Hut 11. I learned on Agnus. A daunting sight! (Each Bombe machine was given a name e.g. Agnus, Kelvin). In those days we were collected in Ford Estate cars driven by Fany drivers (members of the First Air Nursing Yeomanry who took on many of the special driving duties). I was sent next to Wavendon. A lovely house. My cabin had been the master bedroom. A large room with fitted cupboards and a view over the garden and lake. My next stop was in Steeple Clayton in an old, cold and miserable house, working in a barn at Adstock. There we cooked our own food which made a change from working the Bombe. Then back to Wavendon. By this time some Wrens were sent to Mombasa, then Ceylon. (The rest of Ann's story continues under the heading of Wrens Overseas).

ELSBETH CLAY

I was a Bombe operator. We worked eight hour shifts, one week of each and then we had a few days off during which I was SO exhausted that I slept most of the time. I was not very good company for my poor hosts, especially as we couldn't say anything at all about what we were doing. I joined early in 1942 and only stayed there six to seven months. We were billeted in Crawley Grange and then Wavendon. The conditions were terrible, twenty four in one huge room and the food was bad. I got awful boils by my eye and under my arm. At one time they ran out of hot water. A kind woman in the village offered me a bath, but when I got there I found it was a small tin bath that had to be filled by kettles.

The work was quite exacting and very boring. The noise of the machines and the smell of oil was awful. We had to put quite large drums on the front as per the 'menu' and wired plugs in the back. One of my friends got so run down that eventually she was invalided out. I think conditions improved later on.

Elsbeth was later given a commission and eventually went to Ceylon to HMS Lanka as a Cypher Officer.

VERA LISTER (previously BISHOP nee LIDDLE)

I was sent to Station X in 1941 after my initial training in Greenwich Naval College. There were only two of us sent there, I didn't have a clue as to the place or area. There were no Wrens' Quarters then and we both lived with families in the area. My home in England was in West Hartlepool, County Durham. I was a widow when I joined. I was billeted with a young woman who had two children, her husband was in the army. She was most kind to me. At B.P. we ate our meals in the mansion, there was no canteen. The food was pretty awful, but having to work shift work for eight hours at a time, and changing every week, seemed to affect me physically. I could not get used to the changes. This was the reason I requested a move. We were driven into work by truck, open at the back and the exhaust fumes were dreadful. There was no entertainment or get togethers, all Wrens lived separately. As far as I remember I was in Hut 6.

Vera was eventually transferred to Naval Stores at Immingham.

PEGGY ERSKINE-TULLOCH

In March 1942, my husband, a regular Infantry Officer, went overseas with his unit. Having at that time no children, I decided that I would like to join the WRNS. I have to admit that my choice of Service was partly influenced by the fact that khaki would have done very little for mousy hair and a sallow complexion.

I did my initial training at New College, in the Finchley Road, London during which I was asked whether I would be prepared to carry out work "of a confidential nature". I agreed, and was posted to HMS Pembroke III, Station X (as we then were; Pembroke V came later). I was quartered at Crawley Grange, where I spent a few very happy months. I never knew exactly what I was doing during each watch at Bletchley Park, but it seemed to consist of feeding punched cards into a pipe-like machine which ran the whole length of the hut where I worked. Unfortunately I have not come across anyone who worked there with me, so have never been able to discover exactly what we were doing.

Later I went to Steeple Claydon, from where the watches went by lorry with a FANY driver to work on Bombes in the stables of the Manor House at Adstock, a few miles away. It was all quite small; there were only a dozen of us on each watch, and security was provided by a Naval PO and his wife who lived on the premises! We took it in turns to cook, and rations came with us for our watch. One Wren (we have been close friends since those days and are the God parents of each other's children) was at that time very dreamy and was in fact known as 'the cows tail' because she was always last on to the transport and through every door. One day, when it was her turn to cook, she called me into the galley saying she couldn't get the pudding to thicken. Upon investigation I found that the mixture which she was stirring so assiduously was not, as she thought, ground rice but Sanilav powder!

In June 1943, I was posted to the newly opened out-station at Stanmore as a Leading Wren and then in January 1944 to the out-station at Eastcote as a PO Wren and an instructor. Several former Bombe operators whom I have met at reunions in recent years have reminded me how strict I was over the checking of the carbon brushes on the drums at the end of a run on the Bombe. It used to worry me how casually this was often done. I suppose being seven or eight years older than the newly-joined girls, I was able to envisage more easily than they could the consequences of 'missing a stop' – a ship sunk or lives lost on the battlefield, perhaps in the theatre where my husband was, all of which might have been saved. Instructing, on watch during the early hours was no joke: between 2am and 4am was the really low point. I really did, and still do, give those young things full marks. I had to struggle to keep awake (and I understood what I was teaching them!); it must indeed have been a nightmare for them, bless them.

At that time the American GIs arrived, a nice bunch but slightly bemused at first with what must have been a culture shock for them. Their reply to our question of "Why have you come here?" (meaning to Eastcote itself) was, "Why, I guess to free a Wren to go overseas", and this really tore at my heart-strings. At Eastcote we had a competent mixed hockey team, too, composed of Wrens and some of the Post Office technicians who looked after the Bombes. I remember particularly one of them, Eric, a diminutive Yorkshireman whose favourite way of expressing surprise was "Ee, I nearly gave birth to a set of jugs!".

I remember too, at Eastcote seeing one of the first V1s go past our cabin window; we could not at first imagine what this glowing cigar-shaped chugging object could be (but we soon discovered!).

Finally, early in 1945 I went to OCTU, again at New College where I had begun (but I would dearly like to have gone to Greenwich, to where the OCTU moved later). After being Commissioned I joined the Wardroom at Stanmore (where I had been a Leading Wren eighteen months before) as a Watch Officer. My time at Stanmore was uneventful, but I do remember the roll-call of my watch which included, in that order, "Beatt, Wallop and Lynch". Someone must have had a wonderful sense of humour (or none at all!) After the end of the war I remained at Stanmore, during the winter of 1945-6, to help close down the station. This was because my husband was not due home in the UK until March 1946. It was a cold winter, and those of us who were left there slept in Nissen huts with an old stove and not much in the way of bedding or other amenities. We had a working-party of naval ratings to load furniture, and this was the only occasion during my time in the WRNS that I had anything to do with sailors!

For much of the four years neither my husband nor I knew

where the other was: his address was simply the name of his unit and 'MEF' or 'CMF' and mine as far as he was concerned was at first a PO Box c/o The SW District Office (of the GPO) behind the Army and Navy Stores, in Victoria Street. Later he had a PO Box at Bletchley, for me (but says that it meant nothing to him then). At first letters took almost three months, round the Cape of Good Hope, each way, so it was almost six months before a question got an answer! But things improved when airgrammes were introduced in 1942, and still more (a matter of days only) when air letters came in 1943.

In looking back I feel that I was very privileged to have been able to spend those four years in the way I did. I was especially lucky to have moved about so much and to have met so many people, with many of whom I am now still in touch, and some I see again at reunions.

CHAPTER 2

IMPRESSIONS OF PARK AND QUARTERS

BERYL MARTIN (nee BUTCHER).

Towards the end of our training at Eastcote, names of the different Stations appeared on the Notice Board and we were asked to make a choice for posting. Not knowing one place from another, I asked someone standing by, which was the smallest and she replied North Crawley. That is how I got to Bletchley Park!

Memories of the Park are somewhat dim now, but I particularly remember the number of civilians working there, the variety of uniforms one saw, the fleet of buses used to ferry people back and forth (and their Army drivers who were a cheery lot), the MoD police on the gate, and the well-trodden path between the gate and the railway station. One quickly became used to this mix of personnel though, and settled in to the routine of shift work. 'Alarm bells' rang for me one day when I was sent to the local Optician to obtain glasses suitable for wearing under a gas mask. Without thinking, when it came to the eye test I started to read off the letters in the form of APPLE, BUTTER, CHARLIE. DAMN etc. then stopped short, suddenly aware of my mistake. I apologised to the Optician and carried on normally – he made no comment but just acknowledged it. In retrospect, I was a little worried by this slip, but reasoned that he was presumably primed for this possibility, and used to it, and I heard no more of the incident.

The Quarters at North Crawley proved delightful, and we were well looked after there.

DOREEN CLAYTON (nee EYET).

I still look back with a warm feeling of happiness on the two and a half years I spent at Bletchley Park.

Crawley Grange, Gayhurst Manor and Wavendon House were my quarters, and although all three were delightful, my favourite of all was the Grange.

Happy memories by the score come flooding back into my mind with many laughter provoking incidents. My absolute favourite was the time that I went into one of the bathrooms to clean my teeth in the wash basin. An unfamiliar Wren was in the bath and I asked her if she was a newcomer as I didn't remember seeing her before. She said, yes she was, and then asked me what the Quarters were like as she had just arrived. I told her I couldn't imagine a nicer place to be, and of all the perks that we were allowed because we never saw the sea, and we thought the Powers-that-Be were sorry for us! I then said, "The only trouble is that our 3/O (Third Officer) is leaving, which is a great shame as she is very popular and I doubt whether we shall ever be as lucky again." She was rightly very sorry and at this point my teeth were shining brightly and I left my new friend to her splashing.

The following morning at Divisions our Chief said "You know our Quarters Officer is leaving, so she is bringing her replacement out to introduce her this morning." At this point out of the Grange stepped our 3/O accompanied by – Yes, you've guessed it – my bath-time acquaintance!

CYNTHIA WATERHOUSE (nee KIDD)

The breaking of the German ENIGMA cipher messages during the Second World War, and the effect it had on strategy has been much publicized and debated since the secrecy restrictions were partially lifted in 1974. The human side of the story of the WRNS involved in the vital work on the monster deciphering machines has not been told in any detail. It is amazing that none of this information leaked out and if it had, our work would have been rendered useless. I cannot remember it being in any way difficult to keep silent. There was only one thought in everyone's minds, which unified the whole country – and that was to defeat Nazi Germany.

I joined the WRNS in March 1943 and had a strenuous fortnight learning naval etiquette, squad drill and scrubbing floors, etc. I was then drafted to Stanmore were I was trained for Special Duties X, a category known as P5 (Pembroke V). Then I went to Wavendon House near Woburn Sands. The stables had been converted into Wrens quarters – four Wrens to each stable, meant for one horse!

We worked on the Bombes in a hut in the grounds and were connected direct to B.P. The watches were of four week duration, 8-4 first week, 4-12 second week and midnight to 8 am the third week, then a hectic three days and eight hours on eight hours off, ending with a much needed four days leave. The intricate deciphering machines were known as 'Bombes' These unravelled the wheel settings for the Enigma ciphers thought by the Germans to be unbreakable. They were cabinets about 8 feet tall and 7 feet wide. The front housed rows of coloured circular drums each about 5 inches in diameter and 3 inches deep. Inside each was a mass of wire brushes, every one of which had to be meticulously adjusted with tweezers to ensure that the circuits did not short. The letters of the alphabet were painted around the outside of each drum. The back of the machine almost defies description – a mass of dangling plugs on rows of letter and numbers.

We were given a menu which was a complicated drawing of numbers and letters from which we plugged up the back of the machine and set the drums on the front. The menus had a variety of cover names – e.g. silver drums were used for Shark and Porpoise menus for naval traffic, and Phoenix, an army key associated with tank battles at the time of El Alamein. We only knew the subject of the key and never the contents of the messages. It was quite heavy work and I now understand why we were all of good height and eyesight as the work had to be done at top speed and 100% accuracy was essential. The Bombes made a considerable noise as the drums revolved, then would suddenly stop and a reading taken. If the letters matched the menus, the Enigma wheel – setting had been found for that particular key. To make it more difficult the Germans changed the setting every day. The reading was phoned through to the Controller at Bletchley Park where the complete messages were deciphered and translated. The good news would be a call back to say "Job up. Strip machine".

Thanks to the generosity of the Poles in handing over secrets of the early German Enigmas, the brains of Bletchley Park were able to evolve the more sophisticated Bombes. One of the outcomes of this procedure was that the German High Command messages were deciphered in a remarkably short time and during the battle of El Alamein, Hitler sent a message to Rommel which reached Montgomery first, because Rommel's was delayed.

To keep up our morale, we were told that Winston Churchhill was constantly on the line "to his most secret source", and that our work was absolutely vital. We sometimes had news of our involvement in a past achievement such as the hunting and subsequent sinking of the battleship Tirpitz. The pay was thirty shillings a week and it was never clear who was in charge of us as we were detached from the Navy, working under the Foreign Office.

I was later transferred to Gayhurst, another lovely house but in poor condition, then to work in Bletchley Park, and finally quartered in Stockgrove Park near Leighton Buzzard until the end of the war in Europe – always doing the same work.

The people involved in Bletchley Park received an appreciation from Winston Churchill thanking "the geese for laying so well without clucking".

This part of my life had been buried in my subconscious for many years and it was a shock to see the story suddenly shown on TV over thirty years later. But it seems that the Wrens made a great contribution to the Ultra secret which has been described as the greatest intelligence triumph of all time. The fact that the secret remained intact both during and after the war is a triumph of integrity for the thousands involved. Without this priceless foreknowledge of German plans the war could well have been lost before the Allied Forces were sufficiently well armed and trained to achieve complete victory.

LOUISE BARRIE (nee GABRIEL)

I suppose it was all a great adventure for seventeen year olds, having just left school, and to some our first time away from home and family.

In September 1944, Mill Hill opened up again for training probationary Wrens. It had closed for a short time while the 'doodle bugs' were at their height and we, a group of around twenty Wrens, were the first intake.

We went through the usual 'make or break' routine of scrubbing floors, washing dishes, squad drill, Naval tradition, etc. and remembering if we saw an officer at the other end of the long corridor, to stand to attention till she had passed. None of us succumbed to the rigours, and all of us, now kitted out were ready to be sent to our first posting. We were transported by trucks to a destination unknown, and finally arrived at Wavendon House.

A leading Wren took us over to our cabin and told us it was the old stables – more like a large barn and sparse except for our bunks and a chest of drawers for two to share. It was given the illustrious name of Nelson Cabin. We soon found out that we had mice for company and they seemed to enjoy our issue warm vests – we would gladly have given them our 'blackouts', but they had no appeal to them either. Hornets also plagued us. I had never seen them before, their buzzing around then silence. Where had they landed so quietly? – could they be on my bunk? – all rather unnerving. The big double doors rattled and if windy, blew open. It was late Autumn and the leaves were brown and dried. When we awakened we were more like 'Babes in the Wood'.

Fortunately that all changed in a month or two when more Wrens were due to arrive. The cabin was partitioned off, with around eight bunks and all seemed much cosier.

(Note; Mice were quite a nuisance for sometime even sharing ones bed occasionally until Quarters Officer had the bright idea of getting in some cats! G. Page)

The day we arrived we were told by the Second Officer where we were to work. We were to be bussed to Bletchley Park for our eight to four duty and secrecy was the name of the game. Only those of us working in the same hut had any idea what our friends did, nor did we ask.

I was in the Japanese Section and Commander Thatcher, the Officer-in-Charge. The Naval male personnel were from Midshipman upwards and we had a few civilians. It was a happy atmosphere and everyone friendly, but not a 'Jolly Jack Tar' to be seen. I remember 'Tea-Boat time'. A delicacy with our drink was seemingly bread and dripping sandwiches. That did not appeal to me, but I always took my share so that the others could relish their treat.

Lunch-time at the Wrens Mess – aptly named, was not a gourmet extravaganza, especially if en route to your table you had to pass the pails with the plate scrapings. It was not a pretty sight and certainly not an aid to digestion. However, when cash would allow, a trip to the station where the W.V.S. ladies supplied sausage meat and chips, or lucky us, perhaps a corned beef sandwich – such bliss.

'Stand Off' starting at 4.00 pm – off we went to Cambridge and an excellent Y.W.C.A. or up to London maybe to the Proms, The Lunchtime Concert or a visit to the Nuffield Club or Stage Door Canteen. I remember a few of us going to Northampton to hear

Joan Hammond in 'Madame Butterfly' and being adrift (late back). The weather was cold and rainy and the train was very late. We did phone Wavendon and explained our predicament. We all took refuge in the waiting room including Joan Hammond who was waiting for the same train. We all got her autograph and she was very chatty and good and friendly company.

Looking back, I feel it was a privilege to have been posted to the 'Park' albeit as a very small cog in a large wheel, but meeting interesting people, seeing weird and wonderful people and only in such recent years to find out what was really being done at Bletchley Park and that we were mingling with the 'Brains of Britain'.

BETTY MAYALL

I joined the WRNS in May 1944, a month after my eighteenth birthday, and was drafted to Bletchley from Wesley College, Leeds where I had been a Pro-Wren for three weeks. I had dreams of sailing around in little boats and at the very least being able to look out to sea. I had not even heard of Bletchley. Several train journeys and a coach brought a small group of Wrens to Wavendon House – large and beautiful with a lake in its grounds. Forty four of us were quartered in the stable block with constant comings and goings as the Wrens were working a three shift system. There was no quiet and no privacy and our group wondered how anyone was able to sleep.

The next day the transport coach took us to Bletchley Park. It was awe-inspiring: the guards on the gates, the drive up to the great house, the grounds full of huts and large concrete blocks, and I thought how purposeful everyone looked in their different uniforms or civilian clothes. We attended a series of lectures for the next three days which seemed to be punctuated at frequent intervals by strict instructions never to lose our passes without which we could not get into the Park, and never to talk about ourselves or what we did. "NEVER EVER"! Looking back I found this quite easy, and during the war most people seemed to think we were doing some kind of radar job. When the talks ended on the third day I was asked to stay behind with another Wren – also from Yorkshire. We eyed each other up and down wondering if we were incorrectly dressed or had not been looking intelligent enough. But no, we were told we were being delegated to special duties which turned out to be the D-Day and ensuing invasion operations though, because we were at Bletchley, we weren't told about this until they started!

Those who have read books which have since been written about Bletchley Park will know that in January 1944 high level meetings took place there to make plans for the Allies to invade France. Bletchley would be playing a very important part and numbers were dramatically increased to 7,000 by June and "512 staff were trained at the Park to operate the Special Liaison Units accompanying the Allied commanders landing in Northern France". I heard years later that after the 6th June (D-Day) up to 18,000 messages were being deciphered daily at this time.

So, Diana Hardman and I were posted to a small hut in the middle of a lot of bigger ones and we each worked under a Wren Petty Officer with an R.N Lieutenant in charge, three of us on a 12 hour shift. Our leave was cancelled and there were to be no days off. We listened solemnly to our Naval Officers as it slowly dawned on us that we were going to be the only Wrens in B.P being put on a two shift system and doing this particular work. My Lieutenant was a good looking young man called Alistair Macleod who took his responsibilities very seriously. I promptly fell in love with him, but he would hardly have noticed me as my Petty Officer was Elizabeth Moncrieff, and the most beautiful girl I had ever seen.

We had a table each – full of log books and papers stamped 'Top Secret' and 'Urgent' in large, red, capital letters. If anything had to leave the hut the messenger service or telephone could not be used and it would be put into a sealed envelope (marked 'Urgent' of course) and given to me to deliver – and as fast as possible. I did not always know who to, and sometimes I didn't know where I was being sent. I found the night watches eerily quiet though one was all too aware that the Park was a hive of activity. Torches couldn't be used, and the lights in the big house and the huts were dimmed to the point of almost being invisible. One knew, however, that vital work was being done by some of the top brains in the country and I always tried to stop in my tracks and pay my respects to them by dropping a little curtsy as I passed Hut 3 and Hut 6.

And then it all came to an end and I was sent to the Japanese Naval Section where my boss was Lieutenant Gorley Putt, afterwards Senior Tutor of Christ's College, Cambridge. I still have

Wavendon House and Lake 1944

Wavendon House and Lake early summer

Stockgrove Park

Stockgrove Park

The Boathouse, Stockgrove Park

Stockgrove Park 1945

'Men dressed as Seamen' which he wrote and autographed, and I have put the cutting of his obituary, after he died in 1995, inside the front cover. He was very kind to us Wrens in this strange world we found ourselves living in.

By this time I had left Wavendon House and been sent to Stockgrove Park. It had belonged to a Swedish biscuit magnate and was absolutely enormous. All the floors were sprung. There was a magnificent clock tower and an even bigger lake than the one at Wavendon in the grounds with a very grand boat house around which a great many trees had recently been planted amongst great sweeps of heather, which I found rather contrived after my windswept Yorkshire moors.

(Note: Betty sent photographs of Wavendon House and Stockgrove Park also a group photograph taken at Stockgrove Park; unfortunately neither she or I are on the photo, so were probably on duty when it was taken. G.P.)

I remember so clearly the long train journeys through the night. I remember my first Christmas away from home, the first dance and the enduring friendship. Ever determined to get my view of the sea, I ended up in Portsmouth when the Wrens were no longer needed at Bletchley.

I have returned to the Park on various occasions, the most memorable one being the Drumhead service to commemorate the 50th anniversary of V.E. Day on 7th May 1995 to which I went with Joan Tolson (nee Eason). Elizabeth Moncrieff died that same year and I was sent her obituary; she never married and she was still beautiful. Our little hut has disappeared. I sometimes wonder if those strange, unreal weeks were a dream and then I see Hut 3 (now called Spencer House) and I remember and drop a curtsey and know I will never forget.

DAPHNE CHILD (nee BALDWIN).

I joined the WRNS on 12th July 1944 and was sent to Tulliechewan Castle at Balloch, near Glasgow, for the initial three weeks training and then immediately off to Bletchley Park. All I had to be was a reasonable Touch-Typist, nothing else, so duly found myself in Hut 6, working under Mr Harold Fletcher and wondering what on earth had hit me, suddenly finding myself in this strange secretive world! We sat in a row in front of a Typex machine with four wheels on top, touch typing and the finished result came out in a ticker tape strip at the right-hand side, very often just nonsense, but sometimes a proper German message that was instantly recognisable, and whipped away from you very quickly when the "person in charge" came along. It is hard to remember what these machines actually looked like. I was only there for one year. Soon it was May 1945 and VE-Day, and that was when I left to change category to a Writer (G). I spent VJ-Day in HMS Drake and celebrated with hundreds of others on Plymouth Hoe.

I was quartered at Wavendon House and the names of my friends I can really recall are Grace Lunt, Ceri Owen and Barbara Ayres. We were all so very young and naive. Before joining the WRNS I had only ever been as far as London. (My family lived in Hove, Sussex at the time, so you can imagine how I felt, suddenly being thrown into the great outside War-torn World!).

At Wavendon House, we very much enjoyed ice skating on the lake in winter. (Daphne enclosed a photo of herself and friends doing just that, which is reproduced in the book).

Skating on the lake at Wavendon House

DORIS KANDLER (nee SAWKINS)

I joined up in late 1943, but did not get 'my papers' until 1944. Went to Tulliechewan East (Balloch) for Pro-Wren Training (Nissen Huts, etc., etc.). Remember those washed out blue dresses worn with thick stockings and new shoes (or did we still wear our own shoes?) I think I forget that bit. Had my interview! The Second Officer who interviewed me suggested I might want to do this special work – which she said she did not even know any details of and could I put back the chain on my bike if it came off?...was I mechanically minded...? and also that this was SO secret you could NEVER, EVER SPEAK OF IT! (Peril of death). Now could an inquisitive girl NOT go for it?! Also that it would be in London and that the VI's were coming over daily and plentiful – so I should know that. So of course I said "Yes".

I went to Eastcote with about ten or so more girls and was on 'A' Watch, 8-4, 4-12, 12-8 etc. operating a Bombe and alternate on nights sitting in the checking room with an Enigma machine going through 'Stops' and phoning 'Good Stops' through to Bletchley on the 'hot line'.

VE-Day I was in the crowd outside Buckingham Palace with my friends and everyone, thousands and thousands of people chanting, "We want the king. We want the King". We were jammed together like sardines. Suddenly I noticed that a little man had squeezed in beside me and was yelling, "I want the Queen. I want the Queen". I'll never forget how it tickled me to hear him. I am only 5ft. 4in. and he was about the same size and pretty old, and I expect a little bit drunk too!

Myself and many others were transferred from outstation Eastcote in Middlesex to Bletchley after VE day. I slept with others in the converted garage in Wavendon House. Some of my friends slept two to a stall in the stables which had all been lime-washed of course and weren't bad! We had our mess in the house and travelled in the green buses to Bletchley. I worked under Mrs Parsons on Japanese work, "Call Signs" – (I think in Hut 4). We sat at tables all day transposing numbers into groups of five onto slips of yellow paper and what happened to them then I don't know, but some way, by the call sign (point of origin) they could work things out. I still remember the three most frequent main headings which we wrote before the blocks of numbers. 'SATEKO 4, NIMINE, and I think SURABAYO...(The last one doesn't seem quite right, but it was something like that).

Wavendon was a nice place to live, the food wasn't great, ...but the bathroom in the stables was fun. We were all like sisters really, so when two of us went into the double bathroom to bath we'd pull back the blackout curtain that divided the two baths and lull there and soak and chat. Do others remember the 'poem' behind every bathroom door at Wavendon?

BEWARE

Oh, Wavendon WRENS please read, mark and learn
The following facts about 'items to burn'
You may have no fire, no bin, and no brains
But never dispose of such things down the drains
The plumbers refuse to unplug anymore,
It is wasting their time, and losing the war.
So beware all you Wrens, it is quite clearly stated,
The next time it happens you will each one be GATED.
Signed 1st Officer

(Which proves that at least one Wren Officer had a sense of humour! G.P.)

We would often walk up the road to Woburn Sands to a little house on the left hand side, where the lady cooked us eggs and chips (usually that was the menu) and served us in the tiny 'front room'. – it was a real treat to us, 1 shilling and 6 pence I think it was.

I remember we had 'Divisions' out on the drive at the front of the house and could look at the lake and the swans.

I remember the driveway at Wavendon was treeless in 1945 but when I went back 52 years later, the changes were amazing.

I was lucky enough to be at Buckingham Palace on VJ-Day too. We hitched-hiked down and got beds at a Church Army Hostel. On VJ plus two the five of us had a photo taken in Trafalgar Square, which I still treasure although I've lost touch with my friends, Margaret Hayden, Marjorie Hull, Dorothy Middleton, Mavis Bennett, Olive Jennings.

(Luckily I was able to put Doris in touch with some of her friends again and we all met up at the 1999 Enigma Reunion. G.P.)

After VJ-Day we had to remuster to other categories...Not many choices. I went for clothing supply and went up to HMS Quebec at Inveraray on Loch Fynne and then to HMS Osprey on Portland Bill, Weymouth and got my anchor there! (made leading Wren) Wow!! and demobbed August 1946.

(As Doris and others remind us, most of the Wrens were very young and inexperienced in life and relations with the opposite sex. In fact the word sex was rarely heard and if spoken was inclined to be as a whisper. For many of us the first time we were introduced to some of the facts of life was by the Medical Officer at a lecture in our place of training. Most parents could not find the courage to talk of such a delicate subject They found it an embarrassing subject best avoided. The only clue or advice which I received from my mother, was "Keep your legs crossed when out with a boy" which left me extremely puzzled! G.P.)

Doris illustrates this innocence or lack of knowledge with another memory.

One very hot July day in 1945 after we had had our 'delicious lunch' (?) in the mess hut, three or four of us were taking a walk around the lake. It was quite the thing to do, and a pleasant change after sitting writing in the hut. However, one of our number a lively, Scottish redhead announced, "I'm going to tak a wee paddle." She proceeded to divest herself of shoes and stockings, hitched up her skirt and stepped in to the lake. Of course the rest of us were saying, "No, no you can't", etc. But she did – and more than that as she waded on the far side of the bushes. (We were walking level with her on the path of course). She stopped and yelled 'OOH look, a wee balloon, a wee balloon" and proceeded to wave it around in the air!! We were saying "E... drop it down, throw it away" absolutely horrified, and she had no idea what she was swinging around...You know how green we all were! But the rest of us seemed to know instinctively what IT was. We were sure other nearby groups of walkers might have noticed what she had found hanging on a bush!!

(There were some liaisons and love affairs between members at Bletchley Park, although I was not aware of them at the time. Such stories only came to light many years later. This is not to say we young Wrens did not have our fantasies. This ditty sung to the tune of Jealousy went around the quarters. G.P.)

WE KEPT THE SECRET

T'was all over my S.O.P
T'was all over my S.O.P
He was a sailor in the R.N
And I was a poor little innocent Wren.
He gave all his passion to me,
And now I'm a mother – to – be
He was my lover
I daren't tell my mother,
T'was all over my S.O.P
(S.O.P = Sleeping out pass)

I received a further ditty sung to the tune of 'Trees'

I think that I shall never see
A sight as curious as B.P.
A place called up at war's behest
And peopled by the strangely dressed
And what they do they may not say
Nor ever will 'till judgement day.
For six long years we have been there
Subject to local scorn and stare.
We came by transport, bus and train,
The dull, the brilliantly insane.
What were we for? Where shall we be?
When God at last re-dunds B.P.
With Air Force types who never fly,
Soldiers who neither 'do or die'
Land lubber sailors (beards complete),
Long haired civilians, slim, effete!
Such motley throng you'd only see
Within the precints of B.P.
If I should die, think this of me
I served my country at B.P.
And if my sons say, "What did you do
In the Atomic World War Two?"
God only knows (and he won't tell)
For after all B.P. is HELL!

WINIFRED STOKES
I had already been in the WRNS a few months when I arrived

at Bletchley Park – I was first sent on a Radio Mechanics Course, but we proved not to be compatible.

At B.P. there were two practical hazards – the first, living and sleeping so closely with eleven strangers from all parts of the country – strange accents with a completely different outlook on life; at one point one of our group was the daughter of an Earl.

The second hazard was working Shifts – Day Shift, Afternoon Shift and the dreaded Night Shift, creeping in and out of the cabin during the day, hoping not to disturb those who were trying to get some sleep or trying to sleep while those on other shifts came in to change when they came back to quarters. However, it all came together after a while, but only after a heated argument one afternoon in the middle of Woburn Sands High Street, North v South. The northerners accused us, the soft southerners of being insincere, which to us, was only being polite, and we said the northerners were outspoken and rude. "No", they said, "We're just being honest". So it was a good lesson in tolerance for all of us.

Everyone didn't manage to settle down, however, and I remember one young girl from the north of England who was very homesick and kept saying, "Oh, I do miss me Mams golden brown chips".

She eventually got her wish and was discharged. She also gave us a good tip for ironing our shirts – "Slow and smooth," me Mam says, "slow and smooth".

But of course all this petty squabbling was trivial, we were there to carry out the vital job of Code Breaking. Most of us were just the 'work horses' and the best way we could help was doing as we were told as quickly and efficiently as possible. As I had been a typist in civilian life I was told I would be one of the many operators of the Enigma machine. Hours of setting them up with wheels in different sequences as instructed, hoping that the typed up text would appear in German. If, and when, it did the Shift leader had to be notified immediately so that all the messages received on that frequency could be typed up as quickly as possible with the wheel setting that had been used. This was when you felt you really were contributing something.

Although I don't think our shift broke the code on D-Day, I was on Night Shift that night and heard that it had been broken and messages were being sent out by the Germans that our Paratroopers were landing on the French Coast. That was exciting, although worrying as my brother was in the Royal Engineers and I feared that he might be involved. I learned afterwards that he was, but by the Grace of God came to no harm.

The need for complete and utter secrecy was another factor – the all important factor, of course, and we had several lectures on this and signed the Official Secrets Act more than once. We were told that complete secrecy meant just that – we were not to tell our mother, our father, brother, lover, absolutely nobody what we were doing and I know that several of us still find it difficult to say very much. So what did you say when asked what you were doing?, well, you made something up, trying not to sound too stupid.

There was quite a lot of social life, of course, particularly as we were surrounded by American Air Force Camps, with dances either at their camps or our Quarters. There were also trips in to Bedford which wasn't too far away and I remember being lucky enough to be taken to a Concert there given by Glenn Miller and his Band where the vocalist was Vera Lynn. Sadly, I was also at one of the American Camps when news of Glen Miller's disappearance was received. All the American boys were devastated and there was no more jollity or socialising that night, a deep gloom settled over the whole camp.

I was still at Bletchley on VE day but then the strain and stress of the war generally, and working shifts had taken its toll and as soon as the pressure was off I collapsed with a nervous breakdown and was eventually invalided out. But I'm glad I was given the opportunity of being a part of such a vital contribution to the war effort and also of serving in the WRNS. We all learned a lot from each other and despite the miles that separate us, I'm still close friends with one of those "'strange Northerners" whom I met at Bletchley Park.

GWENDOLINE PAGE (nee ACASON)

My experience will be familiar to many ex-wrens. Like most of us at eighteen years of age, my idea on joining the WRNS was to be sent to a port where there would be sea, ships and sailors and some excitement! Instead, after training at Mill Hill, which included scrubbing stone steps and polishing brass taps, I found myself in a transport first to New College in north London where I was initiated into the joys (?) of night watch then two or three weeks later, with packed kitbag and dangling gas mask, on a second

Author outside Wavendon House 2000

The garage had gone and the stables converted to a bungalow. A golf course has replaced the long drive and surrounding ground

transport to heaven knows where!

When the truck stopped I and a few others found ourselves in the courtyard of a large country house, Wavendon House, in the depths of the country and the only glimpse of water was a small lake in the grounds. On asking the resident Wrens, "What are we doing here?", their rather ominous reply was, "You'll find out tomorrow".

The morrow found us boarding a bus transport which deposited us at some iron gates guarded by soldiers, in the town of Bletchley. Here we were told to alight and were ushered in to a room where a Wren Officer addressed us. We were informed that we had been vetted by security and would be doing work of a highly secret nature and must sign the Official Secrets Act. Any mention of our work outside our office would bring dire punishment. After this we were escorted to our various places of work, some to Blocks of buildings and some to Huts.

I consider myself very lucky that I was sent to Block 'A', a much more substantial building that the Huts, where at least the temperatures were comfortable. On each watch there were five Wrens, one of whom was head of watch. There was also a Wren Officer and one or two civilians. My job was to be the indexing of signals intercepted mostly from U-Boats, although there were the occasional signals from other craft if I remember correctly. These signals had already been decoded and translated, so were understood by us all. Each signal as it came to us was copied on to a small white card about 5" x 7" in size and then filed under the U-Boat number. Among messages giving positions or sightings and other technical information, were some of a more personal kind, e.g., "Congratulations to Captain Blank you have a son". These cards were filed into drawers in small chests which one American Officer referred to as "Those goddam shoe boxes".

It did not take us long to pick up the system. Naval discipline remained tight in our particular office and we were always referred to by our surnames, e.g. Wren Jones, or Wren Smith, or in my case Wren Acason. The only time when this was relaxed was on night watch when there were no Wren Officers on duty, but a rather pleasant Naval Officer instead and we all felt less restricted. Between ourselves we Wrens used Christian names and this was picked up by a very new young Naval Officer who joined us for a short time on day watch. He required a certain card and called out to me as the nearest Wren, "Gwen, can you give me the card for U-Boat 159?" There was an immediate hush and we all felt the Wren Officer's disapproval. I handed the card over without speaking and the atmosphere gradually returned to normal. I have always wondered if the young man received a rocket from our Wren Officer?

We met few other workers at the Park, for not only did we have our own canteen for meals, but as soon as our duty finished we were whisked off in the transport back to quarters and so had no opportunity to join in any of the social life taking place that I have since heard about. The only time I entered the Mansion was the occasion when my pocket was picked while I was in the ladies cloakroom. I was not aware of it until returning to quarters I discovered my pay book was missing and along with it my pass to the Park and a £1 note my father had sent me.

A cleaner found my pay book stuffed behind one of the loos in the cloakroom, but the pass and the £1 note were missing. This was a serious loss and meant that for the next few weeks I was obliged to get off the transport at the gates and wait in the guard room for someone from the office to come and recognise me. In the end I had to go to the Mansion where I was fined two shillings and six pence and issued with a new pass. I never knew if the culprit was discovered.

At Wavendon House, my sleeping quarters were in the garage of the estate, along with about 20 or more other girls. The wide doors opened straight on to the courtyard, so that I was delighted when, just before winter set in, I and a friend Barbara were moved to the modern mansion of Stockgrove Park where we shared a beautiful cabin along with six other girls. We were also very pleased to discover the bathrooms to have all modern appliances and even cork-tiled floors. We had gone from the ridiculous to the sublime!

The highlight of my time at Bletchley was when a captured U-Boat was brought into London and Wrens from our office were given permission to look over it. It was an interesting experience to actually be able to board one of the craft we had written about in our signals. One of the first things we noticed was the Schnorkel device which enabled U-Boats to stay submerged much longer than usual and had caused some puzzlement to our people until the invention of the device was discovered. Making our way down the conning tower ladder in tight Wren skirts was a tricky business,

31

especially when we discovered a grinning naval rating standing at the bottom!

The confined space in the actual body of the craft was also an eye opener. It gave the crew very restricted movement. The Captain's bunk was only about four feet long and many of the men in such craft were quite tall. To move through the length of the U-Boat it was necessary to pass through circular hatchways about two feet up from the deck. This entailed hitching our skirt up a little higher than usual to put one leg through the hatch and then duck down to get the rest of the body through; only to come up the other side and find another grinning matelot! They certainly knew were to position themselves!

The more serious side of our visit was examining the torpedo tubes where the torpedos which did so much damage to our shipping were housed and fired. This brought back to us the importance of our work and made our stay at B.P. worthwhile, especially to me, as my young brother was an apprentice in the Merchant Navy. On one point of time I had been able to follow his convoy through the Mediterranean Sea, but of course had not been able to tell anyone of it.

Eventually, the European War finished and with it the U-Boat signals. I was then transferred to the Japanese section where I learnt that most ships were called 'Marus'. The Japanese were nowhere near as methodical as the Germans in their signals and caused more confusion, particularly when one of their ships being sunk, they simply gave the same name to another maru. This meant double checking when indexing signals.

One day I was recalled from leave and told I was to have embarkation leave. (I had volunteered for overseas service when I first joined). This was exciting news for me and I felt that the adventure I craved was about to begin.

(continued under 'Wrens Overseas')

JOAN BAILY (nee READ)

Since my father was already in the Navy – my sister and I decided it would be the right thing to do and joined the WRNS (in any case, it was senior service and the uniform was attractive!!). I was married before joining up (my husband was in the Inniskillin Dragroon Guards) so our surnames were different, so no one knew we were sisters. We did our initial training at New College,

Finchley, which had been a Theological College and still had men's ablution blocks with urinals, and I remember, when on cleaning duty – one young wren walking in and saying, "Oh what dinky little footbaths!".

Having finished our training we were sent off to our various categories. My sister and I went to the unknown "Station X" with mixed feelings of the unknown, mainly apprehension. We were all warned that once at "Station X", that was it. No commission, no getting out of it, and very little leave, and very "Hush, hush" – if anyone asked us what we did, we were to say we were 'writers'. Our first billet was Crawley Grange, in the village of Crawley, several miles from Bletchley. A beautiful Elizabethan House in lovely grounds – but we were away from home, and slightly homesick. I remember finding a 'loo' ("heads in naval jargon"), which was a beautifully panelled, small room, the lavatory itself was raised on a dias, and had wooden arms, rather like a throne, there seemed to be no obvious flushing system, but by means of elimination, I found by pulling one of the arms, the flushing process was activated.

During the first couple of weeks we were entertained by actress/singer Evelyn Laye, and her husband Frank Lawton. We were taken daily by coach to B.P. On arrival at the gates, armed guards checked our passes – then on to Hut 11, and our new job. I understand that this Hut 11 was nicknamed the "Hell Hole", because of the continual noise of the Bombe machines. When a code was broken, there was great excitement and incentive. Though I do remember with sadness, we were unable to break the code before Coventry was bombed.

It was difficult to get used to working in 'watches' 8 am – 4 pm was fine, 4 pm – midnight not too bad, but midnight 'till 8 am took some getting used to, and I am ashamed to say my first night on this watch, I 'dropped off' standing up. At one time I was billeted in Gayhurst Manor in the country outside Newport Pagnell, another lovely stately home, although not as beautiful as Crawley Grange. The owners of Gayhurst Manor were still in residence, Sir Walter and Lady Carlyle, occasionally we caught a glimpse of them, and Lady Carlyle always had a sack tied round her waist, for some unknown reason. It was here at Gayhurst, that having been on night watch, we came off to bed during the morning, but sleep was impossible, and small aircraft were buzzing to and fro. We later found that my sister had decided to sunbathe in the nude on a flat roof! There was not a great deal to do on our 24 hour breaks, because we couldn't always afford the fare to London – and possibly home. More often than not, we would hitch-hike on lorries on the main London Road. The lorry drivers were wonderful – and would stop at various 'pull-ins' (no Little Chefs or Happy Eaters in those days) and insisted on treating us to tea and buns. One truck in particular, I remember, who stopped more than once for us, carried chicken from Cambridge to London – dropped us off in Piccadilly Circus, with our uniforms covered in white feathers! One 24 hour leave we spent in Bedford at a very nice residential house who gave Bed and Breakfast to service women for, as far as I remember, one shilling and sixpence a night. It was the home of Sir Bernard Whally-Cohen, late Lord Major of London.

In 1943, when I realised I was pregnant with my first child, I was told that a glass of milk would be put out daily in the galley for me. Tongues started wagging as to which Wren was 'expecting'. I don't think they ever found out until the day I left. After which, many of my contemporaries went to Woburn Abbey, and thence Colombo to continue the work. All in all, it was a very important part of my life. It was interesting, humorous, and at times sad, but I would not have missed it.

One ex-Wren, who shall be nameless, phoned me to tell a little story concerning a hot water bottle.

It seems that being an old Tudor building, Gayhurst Manor was very cold with little heating in the winter, so many of the Wrens had hot water bottles to keep them warm at night. The bathrooms were at some distance from the cabins. To save an extra trek down the corridors the girls were in the habit of emptying the contents of their bottle out of the cabin windows on to the flower beds below. On this particular morning one girl who had just been promoted to Leading Wren the day before, emptied her bottle out of the window as usual, straight onto the head of Sir Walter Carlyle who was standing below talking through the window to the Wrens in the regulating office below the cabin. She was demoted next day and lost her 'Hook'!

(I suppose the lesson being 'be sure to look first'! G.P)

Gayhurst Manor

WE KEPT THE SECRET

MARGARET ROWE (nee DAY)

I trained on the Bombe at Eastcote on 8 hour watches around the clock. All getting ready to go on watch at the same time. WOW! Then I was transferred to Gayhurst Manor, a beautiful home, which had belonged to Queen Elizabeth I and she gave it to Sir Francis Drake after one of his expeditions. Eleven other Wrens and I slept on double bunks in his bedroom. His name was on a brass plaque on our cabin door and we looked out on to lovely gardens below. We had to walk through a wooded area to the Hut where we worked. When the ground was wet, and our shoes got wet we would get electric shocks when we touched the Bombes, so they got us rubber mats in front and behind the Bombes. The only windows in the hut were high, and one day I looked up at a black haired man peering down at me in front of a Bombe (He was on a ladder). He was an Italian Prisoner of War working on a nearby farm. The noise of the Bombes had made him curious. I ran down the bay and told our Petty Officer, but never heard any more of it.

There was a lovely little church at the side of the Manor House, and one watch when I was not on duty on Sunday morning, I attended services there. My best friend Mary Graham (nee Bevis) and I used to volunteer to pump air into the old organ, it made weird, wheezy noises if we didn't pump hard enough!

We had 'Divisions' in front of the Manor House each morning after night watch – rain, hail, or snow! Our Quarters Officer also made us clean windows and do other chores around the Manor House, but we always did it cheerfully and had lots of laughs! Our right forefinger was always calloused with clipping the 'drums' in front of the Bombes and unclipping them. We used to call the plugs at the back of the Bombe 'Steckers' at first (a German word). I can still remember the phonic alphabet going backwards of course; zebra, yellow, x-ray, Willie, vinegar, unicorn, tommy, sugar, etc. I can visualise what a Bombe looked like, and even though we worked hard we had happy times.

Occasionally, we were invited out to parties and dances at nearby Military bases. The U.S.A 8th Army Air Force was nearby and we got great food at the Officer parties (Much better than ours). I have just watched 'The Glen Miller Story', it reminded me of dancing to his lovely music. The only sad time I had while at Gayhurst was when I got two letters of mine that I had written to my boy friend Norman, returned and stamped on the envelope "MISSING

IN ACTION – BELIEVED KILLED". We were both 21.

Remembering two other incidents while at Gayhurst. In the summer we would go up through the Manor House attic to the flat roof where we sunbathed. The U.S Airforce discovered this and would glide down the wooded incline nearby, switching off their engines and coming over the roof slowly. Did we scatter fast down the attic stairs!! Secondly, we were not supposed to walk through the woods alone when it was dark, but sometimes we were in a hurry after eating in the galley and couldn't wait for company, so ran through the woods alone! Oh, to be young and foolish! That was fifty five years ago.

At the end of the European War, I was transferred to Bletchley Park, and lived at Wavendon House, another stately Manor House. We were transported into Bletchley around the clock, still doing eight hour watches. We were typing 'Top Secret' captured German documents. Many were hand-written and none of us could read German. We were told Mr Churchill got a copy of all the papers – so "no typing errors". We never got any complaints! I asked if my friend Mary could join me there, and she came over the next day. We were happy to be together again. Then later we were transferred to another Hut and travelled every day from Crawley Grange into Bletchley and we were typing already decoded Japanese papers on special form papers. When we arrived on evening watch, if the Oslo Japanese Naval Attaché's paper was not on top of the pile, we would be disappointed. I can't remember his name now. When we signed the Official Secrets Act paper at Eastcote and were told if we did talk we would be "guilty of high treason" and the consequences if we talked to anyone. So we decided we had better not take any chances and only hoped we didn't talk in our sleep. But we always slept like logs anyway! In 1976 when the thirty years of keeping the secret were up, both my parents had died. My father was in the Army in World War I and II and, being an engineer, he would have been intrigued. But I guess it was 'clerical work' of sorts that we did. My twin brother was in the Air Force and my older sister in the A.T.S. (Auxilary Territorial Service).

PHYLLIS SHORE (nee GROVE-WHITE) Died September 2000

I only spent the last few months of 1945 working at Bletchley Park, when I was typing documents which were quite interesting and the 'Boss' was Commander Geoffrey Tandy. Before that, between September 1942 and about May 1945, I was decoding on the Bombes at Gayhurst Manor and Wavendon House.

My most vivid recollections, I think, would be of our life at the beautiful (but VERY, VERY COLD!) manor house, which were requisitioned by the Admiralty. Gayhurst was hugely admired by the Americans chiefly, who were invited to our dances! Also sun-bathing on the roof there and watching the bombers going over to Germany, and then returning hours later with sadly diminished numbers.

Another vivid memory was the hitch-hiking that we all did, especially from Gayhurst as it was so remotely situated that this was our only means of getting from A to B. The thing that impresses me most is the fact that we NEVER heard of any crimes such as girls being raped, etc. and what a contrast that was from all the awful crimes committed today!

I left Gayhurst and Wavendon around the end of 1944 and moved to Stockgrove Park (great luxury after our previous quarters, i.e. tennis courts, indoor pool, etc.) Then from Stockgrove we were taken by bus every day to B.P. where I was in the Naval section in Hut 6 (8?). It was a mixture of Wrens and civilians there and I never did anymore decoding work from then until I was demobbed in December 1945.

Phyllis also remembers having a pass to see the captured U-Boat in London and found it fascinating. She says, "it felt exactly as if the crew had just left – coats hanging up, etc."

All in all, those three years in the WRNS were obviously most memorable and an experience I would never have wanted to miss, and no doubt most of us felt the same way. One thing however did not appeal to me and that was eating a main meal (i.e. supper) at about 4 am when we were on night watch!!

I am so pleased that a Wren friend of mine and I had a lovely private tour of B.P. a few years ago taken by Margaret Sale. It was before it had become a Museum and open to the public and so we felt very honoured! I think we were privileged because I had phoned from Euston saying that I was over from Canada for a short while, and so she took pity on us, and we even got ushered into the kitchen area for tea and biscuits before the tour! I imagine that the Sales and others have worked very hard to have achieved such a rewarding result as the present Museum.

ANNE LEWIS-SMITH (nee McCormick)
wrote her memories in the form of a poem.

OFFICIAL SECRETS ACT
What did you do in the war Grandma?
I forget.
Our ship was sixteenth century stone
which once belonged to Francis Drake
(except the new ablutions block where icy condensation dropped
from concrete walls on naked backs).
He would have been surprised to find
eight bunks with sixteen Wrens who slept
in one high ceilinged, mullioned room
-name Cabin C – where Nancy Someone
climbing down trod on my sleeping head.
Glen Miller and his band came there to play
for dancing in the huge old drawing room.
I jived with Americans, hitched with them,
trod on used condoms and did not understand
-my innocence was unbelievable.
Our mess was once a Monastery
a mere nine hundred years ago.
I wonder did the ghosts of monks
fade to evade the sight of Wrens?
No guiding light outside at night,
stones tripped us, bushes and pine-trees
ambushed the path to where we worked–

At what?
I forget

An extra little memory from Anne concerns wedding dresses. Almost every girl in those days dreamed of a traditional wedding with flowing white wedding dress, but with rationing and shortage of clothing coupons and material, such things were not easy to come by. A few well known people from abroad took pity on our plight and provided wedding dresses for use by service women, among them was Mrs Eleanor Roosevelt, wife of the President of the United States of America, who provided three dresses, one to each of the services – the WRNS, the WAAF and the ATS.

When Anne married in May 1944 she was the first to wear the WRNS dress. She was stationed in Gayhurst Manor at the time and her husband was a flying officer in the RAF.

SYLVIA PULLEY (nee BATE)

I arrived at Bletchley Park in September 1942. Until I was given a rail warrant at Mill Hill, I was unaware that my destination was Bletchley. On arriving at the station, myself and three other Wrens were put into what only can be described as a Black Maria. I imagine this was all part of the need to impress upon us the importance of secrecy. Curious about where we were being taken, we stood on our seats to look out of the little slit windows. We eventually arrived at Gayhurst Manor, where I lived for the next two years. Next morning we were taken to the Park, and after signing the Official Secrets Act, we were taken to the Bombe Room Hut 11 and introduced to the work we would be doing. I was told I would be on duty that night with "C" watch. What with the heat and the rhythmic noise of the Bombes eventually my head fell onto the table, where I was tweezing drums. As you can imagine the P.O. was most displeased, but said as it was my first night on duty it could be overlooked. Needless to say, it never happened again. Colossus was on one side of the room, and I believe at that time was undergoing tests. I only assisted once, as one of the two Wrens who monitored Colossus was ill. When I found myself alone, the experienced Wren had gone to the cloakroom, I just prayed that nothing would break down while I was responsible. At first we were allowed to visit the canteen for a meal while on duty. It was here for the first and last time I ate whale meat! Later we took our food with us. I remember such revolting food as cheese and piccalilli in the middle of the night.

Some of us belonged to the coffee club which was held in the lounge area of the house. The Churchill collection is now in that room. I have to confess that I once slept in that room on the settee. Quite unofficially of course. I came off duty at midnight, and was on leave next day. I had collected my pass at Gayhurst before bussing into B.P. for the four to midnight watch, and had my travelling bag with me. I was able to catch the early morning train. I think they eventually got wise to this practice and didn't issue the travel warrants until the morning of departure.

When Gayhurst Outstation was built, a short distance from the house through a copse, we lived and worked at Gayhurst.

Working on the Bombes could be very monotonous, and the watch keeping very tiring. We needed our day off a week and four and a half days a month. We took pride in plugging up the menu and changing the wheel orders as quickly as possible. Our reward was 'Job Up' and it was your Bombe that produced the answers.

Off duty we led a very pleasant life. One of my fellow C watch keepers, Isla Milligan, commonly known as Aunty, kept a pony and trap at the farm. She would take us into Newport Pagnell for coffee or tea and toast. In return we would help her clean the harness.

There was a dance every month given by the day watch. We always had an American Air Force Band to play, and we in return were invited to their dances and fed on such luxuries as ice cream and fruit by the plateful. Memories of Gayhurst include; Digby's Walk through the Primrose Wood down to the river. Digby was one of the gunpowder plot conspirators; the so called haunted cabin; sunbathing on the roof and a Flying Fortress flying so low that we felt the suction of air; we attended an American Air Force dance a few days later and pinned on the wall were aerial photographs of us sunbathing. I think Second Officer complained and it never happened again.

(Note; I was told by one ex-Wren that Sir Walter was so annoyed at these low flying aircraft that he also went up on the roof to try and take their identification letters in order to complain, but his efforts were confused by the Wrens who muddled up the letters he was trying to read by saying "No, that wasn't an E it was a B, or that wasn't an F, it was an H." They did not want the pilots to get into trouble. In the end he was so confused he gave up! G.P.)

Fire drill was a must every month or so. We had to absail out of a lattice window on the second floor. I remember trying to lift a Wren back into the window when the buttonhole at the waist of her bellbottoms caught on the spike for the latch. We had to crank the engine to pump water from the large tank in the front of the house. If a fire had occurred I think the house would have burnt down before we managed to get the engine running. I also remember pumping the organ and reading the lesson in the church by the Manor. One enjoyable event was being allowed to visit

WE KEPT THE SECRET

Bedford School to listen to a broadcast by the B.B.C. Symphony Orchestra conducted by Stanford Robinson. We had an open invitation for ten Wrens every Friday evening.

On being promoted to Leading Wren I was posted to Eastcote. In those days we sat an examination for promotion. I was placed in Norway bay on "C" Watch receiving menus and wheel orders, etc. (All the Bombe bays were given names of different countries. G.P.) The picture of a Bombe room was taken in that bay by Group Captain Jones and the Sergeant of the Watch Eric Ingham. I was giving out wheel orders at the time. The girl on the right of the picture I think was called Cresswell, but I am not certain. The checking machines at the side of the Bombe were placed there only a short time before V.E-Day, much to the disapproval of the checking Wrens. They preferred the quiet of the checking room.

Off duty we were able to get up to London for the day, and saw many shows with free theatre tickets obtained in Trafalgar Square. We formed the "Sock and Buskin" Drama group with the Americans who had a bay at Eastcote. 'Chalie's Aunt' was produced, with Sheila Mitchell in the title role. Trying to get the Americans to say 'aunt' in the English manner was almost impossible. In a revue we did, I was one of the chorus of can-can girls. Our producer, an American G.I., asked Sir Alexandra Korda for help with the costumes. They were loaned to us plus a team of make up artists from M.G.M. studios. The costumes were splendid, and we wore our Wren black silk stockings. The dance came to a glorious finish with Lilla Tyrer nee Hakins, doing the splits.

One cold winter morning we came off duty and found the regulating staff trying to hoist down bra and pants tied securely and almost frozen at right angles to the flag pole. Divisions were a little late that morning. I think the R.A.F were blamed! I remember standing in the parade ground during Divisions listening to the doodle bomb's (V1's) and waiting for the silence. Never were prayers said more devoutly.

After V.E-Day (Victory in Europe Day) we had the soul destroying job of dismantling all of the drums and leads of the Bombes, the R.A.F. dealt with the heavier work.

(continued in Wrens Overseas).

CHAPTER 3

WOBURN ABBEY

CATHERINE CAUGHEY (nee HARVEY)
Extracts from her book WORLD WANDERER.
Catherine says, "I was stationed for about 10 days at Eastcote and just met a Bombe for two days, then to B.P. and quartered at Woburn Abbey. At Bletchley station a transport met us and we were driven the nine miles to Woburn Abbey, the Duke of Bedford's stately home and the second largest in Britain. If one walked round the outside of the buildings it was a mile. The grounds, which formed a lovely park, had seven lakes, woods and glades, with a surrounding wall which stretched for fourteen miles. The grounds were stocked with wild animals and birds. There were seven lodge gates. The WRNS had commandeered the house, and the Foreign Office had the stables.

Four of us were taken up to the third floor and shown our cabin, which was called Berwick 23. It was one of the servant's rooms up under the eaves, overlooking a courtyard. It contained two pairs of bunks and four small chests of drawers. The wallpaper was dark brown and the floors unstained without carpet, and it was freezing cold with no form of heating.... The bathrooms were still being built, and they did not function for two weeks. The extra 200 Wrens had overloaded the Abbey plumbing, and as all water was polluted there was not a drop to drink. The Abbey lavatories were placed at each corner of the building, and one entered through a green baize door. The walls were covered in red embossed silk, and the pan was of Delft porcelain and raised two steps from the floor and they were warm and private. We called them the 'throne rooms'. Alas I seldom went there as they were too far from the servants' quarters. We had to wait a week before four WCs and three baths were put in on our floor. Even so the water was never really hot....

We entered the Abbey by the southwest doorway, then up the grand staircase to our foc'sle (naval term for sitting room), which was where the family portraits had hung. This was the only room with radiators, and we used to cling to these in winter. Our mess was next to the galley and was the original kitchen and now had Aga cookers. The floors were stone flags everywhere on the ground floor, and they were worn down by centuries of many feet. We ate off scrubbed kitchen tables. We each carried and kept our own mugs, in preference to the enamel issue. The food was meagre, badly cooked, with few vegetables and little meat. Our cabin was so dark and dingy that I got permission to distemper the walls a pale cream and to stain the floor, with Quarters paying for the materials. My grandmother had done a lovely watercolour of Florence and another of a waterfall in Glencoe, and so I pinned these, unframed to the walls to cheer us up..."

In B.P. Catherine's group had two weeks intensive training on the new Colossus machines and then worked week long watches of each duty before having a long weekend off. She continues, "On the Sundays when we were not working from 0900 we had to march the almost two miles from the Abbey to Woburn Village for compulsory Church Parade. The Village church was huge, and the only congregation besides us were a couple of elderly ladies. The ancient clergyman preached against modern youth! I came out fuming, so the next Sunday when they called out, "All Roman Catholics and Nonconformists fall out", I fell out and tried the lot.

The officers at the Abbey had not a clue what sort of work we were doing, and tried to instil naval discipline, and insisted on Squad-drill and trying to make us into Wrens, some were beginning to have nervous breakdowns and other illnesses. This was immediately stopped as by now we all knew too much, and we could never be transferred, and if we dropped out would have to be isolated for the rest of the war. In April, I was granted nine days leave. I was so exhausted I slept for fourteen hours the first night and twelve the second, and it took some time to unwind. When I returned, thank goodness the squad drills ceased for ever, and we were permitted to wear civilian clothes when off-duty. It was another month before they eventually realised that those on night duty needed quiet in the day-time, as we had been disturbed badly by wirelesses playing in the next room.... It took nine months before anything was done about our request not to have the left-overs from the 6pm dinner served up tepid for our breakfast. We came down at 10pm to face steak and kidney pudding which was mostly soggy batter and gravy, with yellow cabbage that smelt of drains. We eventually got our request for cereal and toast...."

An extra duty at the Abbey Catherine speaks of is Fire Watching. "Every three months two of us had to patrol the Abbey at 0100hrs and again at 0300hrs. This involved a good 45 minutes walk each time. We patrolled from the attics to the cellars, a really spooky place with long dark passages with deep recesses leading off them and low arched ceilings. Rumours had it that the Abbey was haunted by a nun! We lived the lives of nuns at the Abbey!"

Later, Catherine and some of her companions "were moved from the attics to a lovely cabin which had been the Duchess's bedroom. It had a high ornamented ceiling, and French doors opening onto the garden. The gilt ornamented inside doors were large double ones with about two feet of thick wall between them. All the state-rooms had these. There was a huge marble fireplace in our room.... We got permission only once to light a fire, with wood we had gleaned from the park. It was so cold that our water jugs froze solid, and I was so cold that I had to put the floor mat on my bunk as well".

Catherine describes her work at the 'Newmanry' in B.P. in some detail. "By now the German High Command began using 'Geheimschreiber' which was much more sophisticated than Enigma, and Bletchley Park failed to break the code.

Bletchley called Geheimschreiber 'Fish'. T.H. Flowers envisaged a machine which would store Fish key-patterns internally and in an electronic form, and would require 1,500 electronic valves. Professor Max Newman from Cambridge University understood and supported Flowers' initiative. Churchill gave instruction that this machine would be given absolute priority, and its construction commenced in February 1943. There were no drawings for many parts, only the designers' originals: no manuals, no questions asked about materials. It was wired and made to work in separate sections and did not come together as a whole until it was installed at Bletchley in December 1943. This amazing machine, the first computer, was called 'Colossus'. It was far superior to the Robinsons and much more reliable, being able to work for long periods. Max Newman built up a large and powerful group, drawing in the best talent from other Huts and from the mathematical world. Colossus worked non-stop for 24 hours for the rest of the war.

It was very hot work as the machine gave out a great deal of heat, but that was a pleasant contrast to the freezing Woburn. I found that bad chilblains on my hands and feet were cured by this warmth. This enormous machine stretched about seven feet high and ten feet wide, and flashing lights and whirring tapes that we fed into them contained the code messages which had been broadcast by the Germans".

As Catherine remarks, it could be very hot in the room working on the Colossus machines, especially in those hot summers of the 1940s. There are stories of the girls taking and hanging their washing around the room to dry and when it became increasingly hot some girls started stripping off in an effort to stay cool. There was an occasion when one young man was asked to deliver a message to Newmanry. He arrived to discover the girls working wearing only bra and pants. He was so overcome, he turned and fled! (G.P.)

"No-one knew what we were doing in 'Special Duties X', and we were told we could not be spared for any leave for five months. Colossus was always breaking down, and we had to wait while the Post Office Engineers came from the hut opposite ours to repair the brute. We learned how to mend the tapes that often snapped. Sometimes I would feel depressed that we were not breaking any codes at all. Yet we were winning through. Colossus II arrived three months later and was a better constructed machine, having 2,500 valves.

I was promoted to Leading Wren, and moved to a small room called Room 12. I was put in charge with Betty Pakenham-Walsh as my assistant. I had been a Girl Guide and had a knowledge of the Morse code. High masts at Knockholt in Kent received the Geheimschreiber code in Morse. They transmitted this over two teleprinters to me, first giving me the letters of the Code setting over the telephone. I had to check these in the Morse which took up 6-8 inches, and then check the two tapes against one another, so as to be sure that neither teleprinter was faulty. The tapes were driven through the machine by sprocket holes and the Morse characters were punched each side of these in five lines. There was a start signal for each tape, which was vital, as it gave the cipher setting for each message. I then rolled these tapes and they went to 'Rob' room as the room with Colossus was called. The previous electrical machines had been called 'Robinsons', after the cartoonist Heath Robinson. Colossus could be programmed according to the starter punches, and by telephone plugs, and the machine set in motion by a hand switch, the tape would whirr around hundreds of different settings working out the decoding at the amazing speed of 5000 characters a second. Often the tape would rotate so fast over the set wheels that it would snap and fly over the room. Colossus II was a much more reliable machine. In Room 12 I found that my eyes ached from peering at all these moving punch holes for hours on end under a neon light both day and night. Some tapes were twenty yards long. The Wrens issued me with metal-rimmed spectacles. Our Huts had no glass in the windows, only opaque mesh. I imagined that this would prevent passers-by from seeing in for security reasons, and also in the event of an air-raid, to prevent flying glass. We had no air raid shelters, either at Bletchley or Woburn. Fortunately we never had a raid, thanks no doubt to the high security measures, taken. (I learned years later that our blocks were meant to be bomb-proof, for the bombs of those days!)

It was about 14th March that a 20-mile travel ban was imposed on us, with a punishment of 80 days confined to barracks should we break it ..... All leave was cancelled. Security was for the preparation for the invasion or 'Operation Overlord'. Life became very intense at B.P. and we knew that the date of the second front was not very far away. Everyone doubled their speed as the Germans were intensifying their preparations also, and many seemed preoccupied. We no longer ate in the cafeteria, and were banned to a hut where we ate alone, and the food deteriorated as the Wrens catered .....

Colossus and the German Lorenz cipher, by Anthony E. Sale F.B.C.S.

The Lorenz cipher system was used by the German Army High Command in World War II. It used an additive method for enciphering teleprinter signals. The method had been invented by Gilbert Vernam in America in 1918, so everyone knew about the additive system but nobody knew the details of the Lorenz machine. In the Vernam system extra teleprinter characters were added to the input plain text character, bit by bit modulo 2. The resulting character was the cipher character which was transmitted by cable or wireless to the intended recipient. At the receiving end, another Lorenz machine set to exactly the same configuration regenerated the same additive characters which when added to the cipher character bit by bit modulo 2, cancelled out the original additive characters revealing the plain text.

The Lorenz machine used 12 wheels each with a mutually prime number of small cams round its periphery, 501 cams in all. The wheels were geared together to ensure a very long repetition period. The task facing the code breaker was to find the patterns of cams round each wheel and the relative start positions to which the operator had turned the wheels before sending each message.

The cryptographic structure of the Lorenz machine was given away by a catastrophic mistake made by a German operator on 30th August 1941.

A special section called the Testery, was set up in Bletchley Park, the Allies code breaking establishment, to attack this cipher, code named "Fish". Laborious hand methods were worked out which showed that it was possible but only with 4 to 6 weeks delay for deciphering each message.

Professor Max Newman had ideas for automating and speeding up the breaking. In March 1943 he approached Dr Tommy Flowers at Dollis Hill, the Post Office Research Laboratories, who started designing and building Colossus to meet Max Newman's requirements for a machine to break Lorenz more quickly. Colossus was working by December 1943 and installed in Bletchley Park over Christmas 1943. It was working by January 1944 and successful in its first trial on a real cipher message. It reduced the time to break Lorenz from weeks to hours providing vital intelligence just in time for D Day, the invasion of Europe on 6th June 1944.

After D Day 10 machines were built and working in Bletchley Park. The Colossi were operated by members of the Women's Royal Naval Service (WRNS). Then at the end of the War eight machines were totally dismantled, two went to GCHQ at Cheltenham. These were destroyed in 1960 together with all the drawings of Colossus and its very existence was kept secret until the mid 1970s.

In 1993 Tony Sale thought it might be possible to rebuild Colossus and started gathering information. Eight wartime photographs and some fragments of circuit diagrams. He decided to have a go and had the basic Colossus working by 6th June 1996 when it was officially switched on by His Royal Highness the Duke of Kent in the presence of Dr Tommy Flowers and many of the

At work on the Colossus

The German Lorenz cipher machine

WRNS, code breakers and engineers who had worked on Colossus during the War.

MERRIE ACTON (nee ENGLAND)

I remember my devoted Ma bidding me farewell at Mill Hill East tube station, whence I made my way to a vast red brick establishment – my first Wren quarters.

One of many fledgling birds, all being vetted over the next three weeks as to their suitability for the tasks awaiting them, I scrubbed enamel mugs with salt, polished and repolished stairs and corridors and then, joy of joy, went with others in a lorry to a farm where we picked tomatoes all day.

Eventually our names appeared on the posting notice board and next day we were driven off by coach into the depths of the country – we knew not where. As dusk descended, the coach sped up the two-mile entrance drive to Woburn Abbey, scattering the parkland deer in all directions. In fact, the then Duke of Bedford, believed to have pacifist leanings, erected notices entreating his wartime guests, "not to take it out on the deer, because of my views on the war!" Often reaching the start of the drive, perhaps at 2.00am after night watch at B.P. we'd be aroused and asked to leave the coach to thoroughly work our shoes through the medicated straw, before continuing on into the estate.

Once inside the Abbey, there was a surge towards the galley (the enormous kitchen) where the cooks had left masses of food and drink. We never forgot to fortify the old police sergeant who stood guard between our half of the building and the other part that was occupied by Foreign Office staff.

'Rodney 10' was an elegant cabin – the antique furniture of course being replaced by rows of two tier bunks. However, the finely chiselled Adam ceilings were there to gaze upon when you couldn't get to sleep because of the noisy so-and-so's on day watch!

In Hut 7 at B.P. I chiefly remember sitting and wading through pages and pages of garbled Japanese matter, excitedly underlining any words and phrases that made sense. This proved easier after a month's diplomatic Japanese course we were given by Henry Reed, the poet – How we all fell for him! Sadly he suffered from T.B. so was unable to join the services. I'm very vague about a machine (the JADE) that was operating in Hut 7 although I do remember doing 'stints' on night duty sometimes with a Wren friend.

Other memories of night duty at B.P. include refuelling visits to the 'Garden Caf' or the NAAFI canteen on Bletchley Station platform where a large old urn dispensed a mixture of tea and coffee to accompany our beans on toast, the tables and chairs heaving energetically as the Scottish Express streaked its way through the little station.

Back off duty to the peace and quiet of Woburn Abbey was a welcome contrast. After a day watch duty in summer, we were able to enjoy Shakespearean play-readings by the side of the lake. On a day off we invariably hitched a lift down the A5 to St. Albans, where we were able to exchange a pyjama chit for some tempting dress material from Green's Drapery Store.

After operations ended, Wren life became very different as most of us re-mustered to other categories – I became a pay-writer at Portsmouth and worked in a small cabin on an old French gun-boat in dry dock. Paying off sailors on their de-mob was very different from life in Hut 7.

I have to admit that it is Woburn Abbey and Bletchley Park that remain clearest in the aging memory!

BARBARA BEACH (nee WOODMAN)

I joined the W.R.N.S. in July 1944. After initial training in Balloch, we returned to Stanmore, Middlesex for placement in various categories.

Those of us with School Certificates or Matric were asked if we would like to be P.5 Wrens, or Special Duties X. We had no idea what this meant, possibly de-coding (all highly confidential). After receiving a basic training we proceeded to Bletchley Park in August 1944.

Several hundred of us were billeted at Woburn Abbey, where we were allocated 'cabins'. Our cabin contained four bunk beds, each covered by a naval bed-spread. The rooms were huge and we were lucky enough to have the 'Flying Duchess's' apartments, complete with a double-loo with baize door and bell for servants. There were also wash basins and showers for us. I remember the great competition for the old baths – only we weren't allowed too much water.

All of us in Whale Island 14 were eighteen and had just left school. Some were society girls with expensive educations, but we all got on well together. We were taken to B.P. by bus (with wooden seats) and worked four shifts which in nautical terms was being on watch. Those of us at Woburn all worked on the Colossus machine. The day-time watch was 8am-4pm, evening watch 4pm-midnight, and night watch midnight-8am. The last watch was a mixture of times. Each shift lasted for one week. At the end of the month there was usually a 36 hour pass and every three months a weeks leave.

The Colossus was a huge machine, there were several in the block. The buildings were known as Huts and inside with all the machinery it was very warm. Because of the Blackout we always had artificial light. The 'Brains' of the Hut under Max Newman were the scientists and mathematicians. We Wrens did the routine work of setting up machines, according to the settings for the day, working through until a clear message in German appeared. Then the messages were taken to the next Hut to be translated. The messages came through from the interceptors on teleprinter machines. There were Post Office engineers on every watch to keep an eye on the machines. Sometimes we heard that our efforts had helped the allied war effort, which was a great lift.

Recently I watched the film 'Station X' and was pleased to recognise Shaun Wylie and his wife. He was one of our top brass and she was one of our Wrens and often on the same watch as myself.

Usually after work we returned to Woburn Abbey. Bletchley was a railway junction so very convenient for trains to Oxford and London. Sometimes a group of us went up to 'Town' to the theatre or ballet. This was at the time of the 'doodlebugs' and later rockets.

During lunch breaks we went to our own canteens or the NAAFI, so we did not mix with people from other sections and of course DID NOT discuss our work. In fine weather we walked in the Park. In the winter of 1944-45 the lake was frozen and several people were skating. Off duty was more enjoyable at Woburn, where we were allowed the full use of the grounds. Many of us took our bicycles down on the train, also our hockey sticks. We often played a game of hockey with the P.O. engineers from the Park.

The only time we had to be careful was when the young stags challenged the old ones. The Duke of Bedford had very special deer in the park. The bus drivers drove very carefully up the long drive.

Every so often we had a dance in Quarters. The Long Gallery at

Woburn was our foc'sle or sitting room. Most of our forces were abroad so the Americans were invited. In return we travelled to their camps – The American Air Force was stationed in Bucks and Bedfordshire. Glen Miller's base was one of them. Most of us went for the food which was delicious after our prunes and rice pudding diet.

When I went on leave no-one ever questioned me about my work, so it was never a problem. As the war drew to a close the messages became fewer and on May 8 1945 our work was finished. I look back on the time at Woburn and Bletchley as a very happy time. We were sent to Gayhurst Manor for a few weeks and then to Stanmore for 6 weeks. During this time we were taken for educational visits to London. Afterwards we were re-mustered and sent to other training. I became a pay writer until 1947. Those due for de-mob went home. Six months after leaving Bletchley I was told I had been promoted to Leading Wren for my work there. Unfortunately I couldn't wear my 'Hook', but I did get some back pay. However I was a very proud nineteen year old.

DIANA NEALE (nee SPENCE)

In 1944 I was called up and chose to go into the W.R.N.S..... I went to the Mill Hill training centre in London for three weeks and when the postings went up I was the only one from my batch to be sent to a place with a code name P.5 (Station X) ..... I was petrified to be going away from the friends I had made – into the unknown! A Leading Wren from the training centre took me to Euston and put me on a train for Bletchley where I would be met. I arrived about 3.30pm and was taken into B.P. and put on a transport bus with about fifty strange, chatting Wrens, still not knowing where I was going! So could you imagine my surprise as we swept into the majestic gates of Woburn Abbey and after what seemed a very long ride we stopped at the front of the Abbey. That evening, after being given a bunk in a 'cabin' – The Chinese Room of Woburn – I had to see the First Officer in Charge who lectured me again about the importance of secrecy in the work I would be doing, and I had to sign a document saying that I would never reveal to anyone the essence of the work.

So by 8am the next morning I was in a building in B.P. again, how lucky I was! I was in a room where there was a long oblong table with both WRNS and Naval Officers and some civilians. At

Woburn Abbey. Photo provided by Irene Griffiths for Bletchley Park Trust Archives. Christmas 1943-July 1945

Barbara Cooper, Pam Cordwell, Jean Bradbridge, Joy Palethorpe? Irene Griffiths, Nancy Atkins, Betty Oliver, Veronica Wright.

a small table near a hand (rope) operated lift I sat with another Wren. This lift was like the ones you see in old houses which were used to send food up from the basement kitchens to the dining room. When we heard the lift we opened the door and took type-written papers which had the decoded German messages typed on them in German. We gave them out to members of the watch on the big table who were all interpreters. When they had translated the German we sent the hand written messages back down in the lift to the typing room. The important part of our work was to check the messages when they were sent back again typed in English against the handwritten translations, in case there were any mistakes. As there were Army, Navy and Air Force Intelligence departments in B.P. the messages were sent to the appropriate departments to be acted upon, but we got mainly Naval information. So, we were always reading messages sent by U-Boat Commanders saying they had sighted a convoy and were about to attack. The Air Force would be alerted and then very often we would read a message from the same U-Boat Commander saying he couldn't surface to attack as the R.A.F. were overhead. That is only one small example, but of course if we did not spot a mistake by a typist in perhaps a degree of longitude or latitude it could be vital. Also we had to verify a typists interpretation of some of the handwriting! We worked in weekly shifts 8am-4pm, 4pm-midnight, and midnight-8am. Many of the messages were teleprinted to the Admiralty.

How I remember that 3am canteen break. It was at 3-5am that it was so difficult to keep awake and I used to say, "When the war is over I shall set my alarm to go off at 3am every night so I can turn over in bed and be thankful I'm not trying to keep awake or have to walk across the wind and rain-swept Park to the canteen to find it was greasy sausages again!" The two Wrens on duty could only go one at a time for half-an-hour each and even then we might have to delay if a code was broken and the messages came flooding in.

The Wrens working on the codebreaking machines hated the job, but there again we were not allowed to discuss each others jobs so that no-one could build up a complete picture of all that went on. Jo Durie was on the machines, but I didn't know her then. She has since said 'the noise was dreadful as they pushed levers and pressed buttons and they worked to a set pattern but had no idea why, and what the end product was'. I was certainly lucky to have such an interesting job even if it was fairly routine.

On the eve of D-Day I was on duty at midnight and I can see now that as we went into the room, Eric Turner, who was Head of the room that night, was standing facing the door as we entered with a huge map on the wall behind him.

"Now before you sit down, he said, "I have to tell you that we are invading France at dawn". And he showed us where the Army and Navy were massed ready and which airfields were at the ready to provide cover. "In view of this you will not be allowed to go to the canteen tonight as you must not speak to anyone outside this room". I can't imagine how two Wrens in the middle of B.P. could have alerted Germany that we were about to invade!! It was a quiet night until the invasion started and then it was all hell let loose with all the German Commanders sending messages to Headquarters and back again.

What really amazes me is that just nine Wrens on Z Watch in Hut 4 read all these decoded and translated messages in English and knew exactly what was happening. What if we had bragged about it?!! Some one on the film of 'Station X' was asked, "Did you find it hard to keep your work secret?" She replied, "If you have been brought up to be honest and truthful and obey rules you did not find it difficult". How true!!

Walter Ettinghausen was in Charge of Hut 4. Diane adds, "After the war Walter Ettinghausen went back to Israel and became their Minister for Foreign Affairs and later their Ambassador to France. When Cliff Mitchalmore did 'In Town Tonight' on Saturday evenings he was going to interview "Israel's Ambassador to France". When he came on I immediately said, "Oh, that's Walter Ettinghausen". So my husband said, "How on earth do you know him?" To which I replied, "Oh, he was in the WRNS with me!" So my husband said dumbfounded, "What on earth was an intelligent man like that doing in the WRNS with you?" "Oh just clerical work", I said.

DOROTHY DU BOISSON

I joined the WRNS in April 1943 and did my training at Mill Hill. When my clearance came through I was posted with others to Stanmore. When we got there they were not ready for us to go on watch, so we spent our time between lectures and squad drill cleaning cutlery, mending coconut matting, and cleaning paint off windows. In the meantime a job came up in the country, and during the interview in which they could tell us nothing about the work, the ability to amuse yourself when off duty seemed to be the criteria, and so I went to Bletchley Park.

Sixteen of us went, eight one week and eight the second week. I was in the second week. We went to a section called the Newmanry which was just starting up. On our first day Mr Newman came, as we thought to tell us what we would be doing. He was a very shy man and walked up and down in front of us looking at the floor and talked about a machine with ten wheels, we were none the wiser when he left. He was under the impression we had been told what the work was and he was giving us more details.

When we arrived we were quartered in a small village rectory in North Bucks and as there were only eight of us we were really spoiled. Then the sixteen of us were sent to Woburn Abbey, the first to arrive there and we rattled around like peas in a pod. It was a vast empty house, bigger than it is now, very cold in winter, only electric bars in what was the picture gallery. Then, the Duke of Bedford was scared of fire, the Abbey being burnt down in the past ..... There was a notice on the wall of the first cabin I was in saying 'extinguish the candle before retiring'. Consequently we had to take our turn at fire watching, and nobody enjoyed going through the underground passages in the middle of the night.

At one time I was in a cabin in the North Wing overlooking the Monks Graveyard when one of the girls declared it was haunted as she had seen one of the monks fly through the window! Some girls refused to go up there after dark, so the lights were kept on all night.

The Newmanry was run by mathematicians and linguists all extremely clever men, we were there to work the machines. All the messages came on tape from Knockholt. They were wound round a wooden spool and the first thing we had to do was join it into a loop to be wound round the wheels of a machine we called Heath Robinson as it looked so strange. We had great difficulty getting the join to hold as the machine went so fast it split the join and the tape would fly all over the room. Eventually the problem was solved. Then along came Colossus, even bigger, faster and more reliable, to be followed just before D-Day, although we did not know it at the time, by an even better version.

The Section was a very happy one and very informal, except for Mr Newman everyone regardless of rank was called by their Christian name, much to the surprise of an American Naval Officer on his arrival in the Section. We eventually grew to quite a large unit and for some girls it was very boring just putting tapes on and off machines, so once a month we had a little talk to tell us something of what we had achieved.

At Woburn we were very isolated, it took about half an hour to walk to the gate, but I think everyone enjoyed being able to roam all over the wonderful park. Life there was informal we were only available once a month for Church Parade or Squad Drill. I remember one drill very vividly when the Officer taking the drill suddenly said she had something to do and called me out to take the drill, I was petrified never having given a drill order before and all she said was, "Don't march them into the lake".

When the German war finished, so did our job and it was thought we might go to the Far East to do the same to the Japanese, but it fell through because we were told we had captured all the codes we needed and the war would end soon. One day to celebrate the end of the war we all went to lunch together and shut the front door. Of course on our return no one had a key and so I learnt how to open a Yale lock with a hairpin!

Bletchley Park was a wonderful experience and I met people I would never have done otherwise, and it gave me confidence and assurance I think it would have taken some years to acquire.

We returned to Stanmore for demob and there was a bit of feeling as we had not got promotion to Petty Officer, but it soon passed, and so back to civilian life and tight lipped for thirty years!

ENID SEAGROVE (nee FEAR)

I arrived at Bletchley Park in 1944 as a newly-fledged Wren, having spent two weeks in a training depot in Mill Hill, North London. Living Quarters were in the splendid Woburn Abbey, sharing a cabin with a dozen or so other Wrens and several nocturnal mice. A recce in the surrounding parkland revealed, incongruously, a light aircraft, subsequently explained many years later as being the means of transporting agents to occupied territory after training in the rear part of the Abbey.

In Bletchley Park I worked in Hut 4 where following decoding, incoming enemy signals were translated into English prior to being teleprinted to the Admiralty. Each of three watches had six translators comprising a mixture of civilians, Naval and Army personnel plus three Wrens, our main job being to check the translated signals with the teleprinted copies. Content and volume of signals varied considerably, sometimes vital, sometimes apparently unimportant, but all requiring evaluation by the Head of Watch and others.

I worked in the Park for a year, during that time changing my living quarters to Stockgrove Park, a much smaller country house in Leighton Buzzard. Shortly after V.E. Day the opportunity arose to volunteer for overseas service, the destination being Ceylon, as Sri Lanka was then called. The work would still be in the same category but connected with the war in the Far East. (Continued under 'Wrens Overseas')

RAE CROSS (nee JOHNSTON)
sent a piece on her return to Woburn Abbey.

I too served in category PV and during the years 1943-45. I was quartered at Woburn Abbey.

In 1957 my husband, small son, and I decided to visit Woburn (it had then become a Stately Home) for the day and after purchasing our entrance tickets – much to my surprise – my ticket happened to be the Half Millionth visitor to the Stately Home. I was informed by the Security Guard that if we cared to follow a certain Police Car to an area behind the Abbey, the Duke would be waiting to receive me! What a surprise arriving back at Woburn after a gap of so many years to be treated so royally. After introduction to the Duke, he gave me a warm welcoming speech as his Half Millionth visitor and presented me with a silver powder compact and a large bouquet of flowers. After thanking the Duke for the gifts I told him that I had been quartered in the Abbey as a Wren during the war years, whereupon he remarked upon the coincidence and thought that "it could not have happened to a more appropriate person", adding, "bet you know my house better than I do. Come on let's go and look at your old haunts".

The Duke was most gracious and easy to converse with and seemed very interested in my small son, and he was not slow in offering to buy him an Ice Cream from the Ice Cream Stall even queuing up with everyone else to purchase one to give to him. The

WE KEPT THE SECRET

Duke asked if there was any particular room I would like to revisit, and I remembered asking if I could see the Chinese Room again (this was a large cabin during our stay there, holding some 10 or 12 double decker bunks). Imagine my surprise to find the Chinese Room behind the roped off area – telling us it was now occupied by the Duke and his family as private quarters. However, the Duke was quick to remove the barrier and asked me to lead the way.

The Chinese Room of course, had since been cleaned and made shipshape (the precious wallpaper had been covered with hardboard during war time), and it was now restored to all its splendour and the wall covering revealed to me for the first time. We also went up to the Nun's Gallery (here again the rooms had been used as cabins, but this too had since been made into private flats. I hardly dare ask to see the bathrooms (some dozen in number), where the baths were mounted on stepped pedestals for modesty reasons, and nicknamed by us as THE TOMBS owing to the fact that the baths were made of tin and if bathing and one's arm struck the sides a loud clanking noise would ensue.

We then went to see the Long Picture Gallery now restored with all its beautiful priceless pictures, which had been used by us as our foc'sle. Here we had held our dances, and it was hard to remember how it was way back without any pictures.

All in all we had spent almost two hours being escorted round by the Duke and he took his leave of us in the private gardens – not before picking a gardenia and presenting it to me. He told us to walk around wherever we wanted and just to enjoy being back at Woburn.

On our way home our son asked if "we had been important people" as there had been so much fuss made of our visit, but naturally he was too young to realise just what a momentous day it had been for me. Next day it was a thrill to read some write-ups in the daily newspapers of the coincidence of our visit to the Abbey, especially reading in the William Hickey column in the Daily Express under a heading ..... A Wren Comes Home. I must say the visit had felt just like that.

DOROTHY SMITH (nee ROBERTSON)

I graduated MA at Aberdeen University in June 1942, my degree being a general one, with Ordinary French and Advanced German included. Two of us, keen to join up in the Women's Royal Naval

Service, went down town literally the following day to sign on, hoping that it would not be long before we were called up. For days, weeks and months I ran to the (in those days, three times daily post delivery!) front door, hoping my papers had arrived and as time went on, it seemed that they simply did not want me. I had no job, so filling in the waiting time wasn't easy. However, the Great Day dawned when a letter arrived for me, asking me to report to WRNS Mill Hill in London, in January 1943. I was simply thrilled. My mother too was glad for me, but my old fashioned father, wishing to keep his youngest daughter at home, threatened to write in protest to the Admiralty! I was horrified...

The depot at Mill Hill was the Cancer Hospital, converted to receive hundreds of Wren recruits, and I mean 100s...they were everywhere in this huge modern building. We had to line up to give our names, special abilities, and so on, and I suppose that this was when we received our service number, mine being 59,516. Then one after another we were submitted to the indignity of having our hair combed!! We were very amused, never having had such an experience before.

Mill Hill kept us for two weeks, during which time we all slept in huge dormitories, each having the name of an RN ship. After breakfast we had to report for 'house duties' and for some unaccountable reason, another Scots girl and I in our group were always made to clean the baths, loos, etc. on our floor. Off we trundled with buckets and cloths, in fits of laughter. The girl, a pretty little blonde called Deva Cayzer from Perthshire, asked me to post a letter for her one afternoon when I was going 'ashore' (i.e. out), and I noticed that it was addressed to Lady Cayzer, some castle or other, Perthshire. When I mentioned this letter to my parents they were most amused, realising that Deva belonged to the very wealthy shipowning family. After Mill Hill I lost track of Deva until soon after the war when I read a long account of a very fashionable wedding in the Daily Telegraph: At St. Margaret's Westminster, the Hon. Deva Cayzer...to...plus lots of bridesmaids, etc. So much for our initial training with buckets and cloths at Mill Hill!

One day I was sent alone to the Admiralty to have a test in German. Of course I was terrified but found the atmosphere quite informal, and I must have passed because soon I was sent to RNTE Southmead, Wimbledon where I did, with a few others, an intensive and very exhausting course in Special Duties (Linguist) which at the time was highly secret and we all had to sign the Official Secrets Act. It has been exposed in recent years, I suppose after the 30? year ban. We had to learn, among other things, shorthand for certain German Naval terms and take down rapid messages in German from headphones. There were some ten or so of us, all worrying ourselves stiff that we'd fail the finals. On the exam day, our examiner/transmitter, a rough old naval chap (TH Hatch) who had never fully accepted the idea of women in the Navy, transmitted to us in German R/T (i.e. Radio Telegraphy or speech) from the next room. When he came in to us afterwards, we all said, "Oh Mr Hatch, how was it? Did we do alright?..." In sly humour, grudgingly, he replied, "Bloody perfect..." We were most amused and much relieved and glad to know that we girls could cope as well as any men. (This was confirmed after the war, that women were equally as good, and sometimes better, than men at detailed jobs).

While at Wimbledon we were billeted in a very pleasant house, "Rosemead", and did our training in another house nearby. Many an evening off we would go up to the West End, and fearful that we would be back later than the regulated time, we would ask the other girls in the dormitory to make a hump of kitbag, or suchlike, in our bunk, so that the duty officer Wren at lights out would think one was in bed. There was a very handy French window in the room and we could sneak in there late. I remember once, on seeing the huge lump in my upper bunk, (I am 5' 2") feeling amused that Second Officer should take such a hulk for ME! It was no joke going out at night in those days since in the blackout one walked from the bus (at Tibbit's Corner) in complete darkness, a thing I would never do today, but during the war there seemed to be little or no danger.

From Wimbledon I was posted alone to St. David's in Pembrokeshire, HMS Skirmisher. Although I came from Scotland and had often been in remote places, I still remember my feeling of desolation as the train from Paddington carried me further and further into the wilds. St. David's is, or was, a tiny village on the south west tip of Pembrokeshire and the Wrennery was a sort of converted lighthouse with a circular room at the top, windows all round, this being our watchroom. Nobody other than ourselves knew that we had VHF sets (2 per Wren) and D/F equipment, and indeed, Chief Officer from Milfordhaven when visiting, was not allowed inside it. Two Wrens manned the sets, two each, continuously, one for German R/T the other for W/T. All this of course was top secret at the time. We also had to take it in turns to "sleep" a night in a wired-off hut in a nearby field where, if necessary, one had to take a D/F bearing on any signal that was sent through to you from the watchroom. It was quite creepy being in the hut on one's own, and I remember once when the watchroom phone went, leaping out of bed, shivering in my nightie, plunging into a large puddle beside my bed and then trying my best to take a bearing on a signal – panic stations! This small Wrennery of twelve Wrens (all Petty Officers and Chief Petty Officers) with one Third Officer only, Mrs Chamberlain, a French woman married to an Englishman, was a very happy station in spite of the fact that we were miles from everywhere and everything. We went on beautiful walks along the coastline and the deserted bays and Spring in South Wales in 1943 seemed to start earlier and look lusher than anywhere else I had seen. Of course a romance with one of the theological students evacuated with his Llandaff College from Cardiff may have had something to do with that. From St. David's I was suddenly drafted at 24 hours notice in June to Withernsea, a dreary secondrate seaside resort on Humberside. At first I hated it – the flat colourless countryside really was depressing and the rolls of barbed wire in front of our Wrennery on the beach (quite inaccessible unlike those in Pembrokeshire) made it more so. The only form of amusement was a large dancehall, but we didn't like it and seldom went. However it was here that I met two more P/O Wrens like myself who were to become lifelong friends – Sheila Cassie from Edinburgh and Anne Robson from South Africa. We three were later to spend almost two years together in Ceylon (HMS Lanka). At Withernsea, I can remember while on watch with my headphones on, hearing German bombers swooping down over us on their way to bomb Hull with the pilots yelling to each other frantically and excitedly, their call-sign being flowers, – for instance, in German: "Hello Hello, this is Daffodil, this is Daffodil. Calling Tulip...etc." Very nasty. We knew that the WAAF (Women's Auxiliary Air Force) would be covering it, so we did not log it in detail. Hull was indeed badly bombed.

After the summer of 1943 in dreary old Withernsea, two or three of us SD P/Os were posted to Scarborough – totally different again.

Here was a high class summer resort of prewar days, now stiff with service personal of all sorts, there being umpteen aerodromes all round it. It was the biggest base that we SD girls had ever been in, since up to now we had been spoiled in small pockets of 12 or so only, with just one 3/O. Now we were plunged into a large set-up with lots of red tape, squad drill (what's that?), parades, rules, no privacy, and lots of Wren officers everywhere telling us what we should be doing. Work was no longer just upstairs in the top room of the house; now we had to go in buses to a large W/T station outside the town. All I can remember about it was the huge watchroom and the enormous mugs of thick strong cocoa brought to us twice a night on watch by sailors – just the thing to make one sleepy, I thought, when to fall asleep on duty was every Wren's nightmare. We had to keep reading notice boards at Scarborough, and we were billeted out in erstwhile summer lodging houses in town, where, that Autumn, the cold winds used to whistle though gaps in our bedroom wall! Anne Robson and I were billeted with a Quaker landlady who was so strict that we had to beg to fill our hot water bottles every night. UGH.

At Scarborough we learned that volunteers from our (Lingquist) category were wanted to go overseas to Ceylon, so of course Anne and I were immediately interested and sent up the necessary forms. At first we were terribly disappointed as only six were chosen – not us – but some weeks later, we two were accepted in the next batch of six. What a thrill! Having been an infant in India, it had been a lifelong ambition to go back, and here, in the war, it would be fulfilled...I could hardly believe my luck. But of course it was highly secret and not even one's family could be told. My parents would have been, and indeed were later, almost as thrilled as I, for they had retired a few years before the war from India.

My father knew Ceylon from his batchelor days with the Mercantile Bank of India, but most of his 30 years in the Bank were spent in India itself; my mother spent 15 years with him in Karachi and Bombay. So one could only tell people that one was 'going overseas' and not even when. Eventually, Anne and I were sent from Scarborough to start our course at Bletchley Park in Buckinghamshire and were billeted with some 598 other Wrens – all doing different jobs about which none of us knew anything, as no one was supposed to talk about work during service life – in the huge mansion, Woburn Abbey, which belonged to the Duke of

Bedford. During the war it was Spartan and we really hated the place. It was January and February, 1944 and the cold winds blew and blew and ice froze up the water supply and the rooms were so vast that one was always frozen. The six of us on this course slept in double-decker bunks in what must have been a very grand room normally, as there was brocade on the walls and a beautiful plaster ceiling, and a lovely step-out window into the Orangery. I was on a top bunk and so cold that I thought I'd be blown out of bed at night with the breeze! Furniture, etc, was of course the barest. There was a very old-fashioned W.C. like a throne room where one had to walk some four yards just to sit down on a wooden throne – always freezing – and the water sometimes literally. We used to laugh lots...

After breakfast every morning, several coaches awaited us Wrens at the front door of the mansion and we were driven a few miles through the park, to Bletchley Park. I think there was a large house in B.P, but all over the Park were huts for various activities connected with the war and no one had any idea what went on in any of them but their own. It has been very intriguing to read so much about B.P. in recent years, now that the press is free to publish it... it was all so secret in those days. Our own course was to learn Japanese Naval language and we had two instructors: one a brilliant young man, Angus Wilson who, after the war became keeper of the Library at the British Museum or suchlike and a senior book critic. The other was a Lieut.Cdr.RN Dugmore. Angus Wilson used to mince into the room swaggering, and wore what were outrageous clothes in those days: a bright yellow waistcoat, a red bow tie and perhaps corduroy trousers; his nails were bitten right down to the quick, he chainsmoked and he had a horrible cracked sort of laugh! Anyway he was extremely clever – that's why he was there, no doubt cracking Japanese codes when he was not teaching us. The other Tutor, Lt.CDR. Dugmore ("Duggie") was young, blonde, and handsome.

Coming home every evening to Woburn Abbey, we seldom saw it in daylight, so the vast stone-flagged kitchen and ground floor rooms and corridors seemed forbidding and cold to us. It was easy to get lost just walking from our bedroom to a sitting-room. As there was said to be a curse on the Abbey and two old buildings had been burnt down in the past on the same site, Chief Officer ruled that two Wrens must patrol the whole 3-storey mansion in two hour shifts every night, since incendiary bombs were also a hazard. This rather unpleasant duty had to be done by us in rotation, and of course, when my turn came, not only was it the midnight-2am patrol, but my partner fell sick and at last moment on the very evening, I had to try to find a substitute...(surely she should have done this?). Everyone I asked had either just done it or was going to do it soon; the thought of doing it alone was scarifying, so I went to my officer and reported the crisis whereupon she told me I'd just have to go ahead and do it alone! At 10pm as everyone was going to bed, all 600 Wrens in this huge square mansion seemed to disappear behind bedroom doors, and I decided to do a 'recce' on my own. Along l-o-n-g- straight corridors with windows on one side looking into a central courtyard, now dark, and against the inner wall enormous old chests containing documents relating to the last (1914) war – so we were told – I walked quietly, passing on the ground floor the "Queen's Room", the "Prince's Room" and I think the "Indian Room", whose double doors sucked with the draughts of the winds outside and whose mystery, being permanently locked, always gave us the shivers. Years later I was told that the family treasures were stored inside...naturally, but at the time, it was spooky. Coming to the Grand Staircase, I looked up, the huge paintings and portraits on the walls, and began to climb. At the first floor I was aware that a woman with long hair and wearing a long dress was standing looking down at me from the very top of the staircase on the third floor. I kept walking upwards, not looking at her but remembering that there was a room at the top called the 'Nuns Room', said to be haunted. I felt more and more nervous as I ascended...it was dark, cold and late and no one seemed to be about except me and this figure. Now I had to turn along the landing of the second floor and do my rounds...When I came back to the Grand Staircase, the figure was still there looking downwards and I became quite nervous as I now had to climb upwards towards her. Finally, walking more slowly with every step, I looked up at her – and saw that it was one of the Wrens in her dressing gown, her long hair hanging down her back! I had to pass her at the top and she told me she was waiting for a friend to come up to bed! But such was the atmosphere of the building, Woburn Abbey, that it was easy to imagine ghosts in those long corridors. I knew that the family had had a very unhappy history, so that didn't help.

Many years later, in the 1970s, I read a letter from the present Duke of Bedford in the Daily Telegraph, in which he described his reactions to opening his home to the public in postwar years. (He is, in fact, not the same man who lived in the grounds of the Abbey during the war and whom we heard, was a pacifist and cursed everyone of us for taking his home!). So I wrote to the Duke of Bedford, mentioning my time as a Wren in his home and asking him if there was any truth in the legend of the ghost. He replied in a charming letter, saying that indeed it was so, and that they had had the room exorcised, but that there was still a very chill atmosphere around it.

One other factor that added mystery to the place was the fact that there was a small aerodrome in the grounds, and driving past in our coaches to work, we would see RAF personnel with their Alsatian dogs patrolling it. It was not until after the war that we learned that Winston Churchill and the War Cabinet frequently flew in to have meetings in the mews buildings.

(Continued in Chapter 8 'Wrens Overseas')

CHAPTER 4

Spies?

JOAN UNWIN.
Early Spring 1944.

It will be remembered by readers that this was a very sensitive time. I, a lowly Leading Wren was going to my home in the North East of England for a spot of leave. The corridor train stopped at all the main line stations en route north. I was the only occupant until two 'Jolly Jack Tars' entered the compartment.

"Aha, what have we here", said they almost in unison!

"Help", I thought, they are sure to ask me awkward questions, I could tell!

"Where was I going, what did I do?" – "Careless talk", said I, that made it worse!

They noted my rank and after much merriment, "What did I do" came the question again.

"I am a secretary", said I (which was true).

"But no category badge" they choroused and then "Perhaps she is a SPY!"

I thought it was time I made my exit of compartment and carriage. I managed to alight at the next stop and board further down the train – in those days the length of the main line trains were immense. When the train reached my destination – Newcastle-on-Tyne – I waited as long as I dared (as the train was going to the far north of Scotland) before alighting. Thankfully I did not see them again. – PHEW!

Peacetime – in the 1970's

My husband John and I had been married for 30 years or more when one spring we visited a Stately Home in the South of England, where we lived at that time. The Magnolia trees were in full bloom. John said, "There were two such lovely Magnolias where I was stationed for a time during the war". Oh said I "I knew two such lovely trees too – beside a lake." "Really" said John – Same lake, same Magnolias at Bletchley Park! In all those years we had kept the secret from one another!!

JOAN COLE (nee VICKERS)

My memories of Bletchley Park, setting up the Bombes and the "Jobs Up" cry will be much the same as everyone else I expect. BUT I did catch two spies! I was sitting in a cafe in Bletchley one day drinking a coffee, when a young man came to the table. "May I join you?" he said, "How about another coffee?" "Thank you", I said. He sat down and chatted a bit. "You work over there don't you?" he said pointing towards the Park. "Yes", I said without thinking. "Bring me what's in the waste paper basket, won't you" he said "Big box of chocolates in it for you." "Oh I said thinking fast "Cadbury's?" "Of course", he said "Now where will you meet me?" We arranged a meeting place and I arranged for the Military Police to keep the appointment!

The other incident happened when I was waiting for the train to Bletchley on a London Platform. A group of Army Officers were also waiting on the platform, and one of them came over to me, a Colonel. "Are you going to Bletchley?", he said, without thinking I said "Yes" then of course I realised I should not have said so! "Damn" I said to myself. So I went over to a WRNS Officer and acknowledged my mistake. She summoned the Military Police, "Come with me", he said "Who was it? Point him out to me, but carefully!" So I did. A month later I was summoned to the office and told that the man I had pointed out was a spy they had wanted for a long time! Nice of them to let me know – and what a small incident to have betrayed him! It shows the value of what was hammered into us – never say where you work and if you do make a mistake, acknowledge it instantly!!

I went to Colombo later – a rather grim voyage, Aden for three days, first convoy through the Suez Canal – then Mombasa and across on the Khedive Ishmael – due for home leave after six years – She was torpedoed next run.

Note. The KHEDIVE ISMAIL a British Troopship – 7513 tons. Deployed in the Mediterranean evacuation of Greece and Crete in April 1941. She was one of thirty ships sunk in the Indian Ocean during the months of January, February and March of 1944, by the sixteen enemy submarines operating in that area at the time. She was struck by two torpedoes fired by the Japanese submarine I.27 at 9.05 am on the 12th of February 1944 just south of the Maldive Islands when bound for Ceylon. She sank in two minutes, with the loss of 1200 British/U.S. troops and service women, and 150 crew.

(Source; Royal Australian Navy 1942-1945 by Hermon Gill)

(I was told that only two Wrens from the whole WRNS draft were saved from this disaster. G.P.) Stephen Harper gives the story in his book CAPTURING ENIGMA.

CHAPTER 5

THE JAPANESE SECTION HUT 7

Gathered by MARGARET HENDERSON (nee BROWN)

Margaret joined the WRNS in November 1943 and was at Woburn Abbey, and Wavendon Park Farm until after VJ-Day.

Hut 7 in Bletchley Park was one of the few buildings there where people were NOT trying to decode European languages. It was known as the Japanese Section...'Known' is perhaps the wrong word because as young recruits to the Foreign Office or WRNS plus a few from RNVR we, quite rightly, took our signing of the OFFICIAL SECRETS ACT very seriously. Many of us have spouses who did not know for more than thirty years what we did there. Unfortunately we were so geared to not speaking about our work that many of us can remember little, but some more than others. What follows is a rough collation of information from collegues who were there.

There have been Hut 7 Reunions in London since 1946, light-hearted, friendly affairs, and obviously for at least the first thirty years, work could not be mentioned. These Reunions have continued every year, 1998 being the only exception.

Less than a year ago I was asked if I could gather together information about Hut 7, and with tremendous co-operation I now have a good list of names, details of our work, where we lived and our leisure time.

It now seems clear that the Wrens had a better way of living than the young people employed by the Foreign Office, who were billeted with kindly folk often in very simple homes. It sounds as if the 'civilians', as we Wrens knew them, were often a little lonely when off duty due, perhaps, to the fact that their hosts knew nothing about what they were doing and therefore maybe thought they should have been in 'useful war work'. However, one young man asked his landlady if he might play his flute, and she agreed saying that she liked some type of noise and did not care what it was!

Very occasionally some of us in the WRNS wished we could be

alone, but not often. Many of us after initial training, were posted to Woburn Abbey (400 Wrens stationed there) where the going was tough and often very cold, but we were happy.

Here are some 'quotes':

"Often about 2 am after night watch at B.P we'd be aroused and asked to leave the coach to work our shoes through medicated straw, before continuing into the Estate". There had been cases of foot and mouth disease in cattle, and we were told this would prevent it spreading to the famous herd of Estate deer!

"One strange aspect was that three Wrens were detailed each night to patrol Woburn Abbey as a fire precaution. A separate cabin with three very creaky bunks was provided and on these occasions, the Wrens were given trousers to wear and hooded torches. The first round was from 11 pm to 1 am; the second from 1 am to 3 am and the final round from 3 am to 5 am. This was an eerie experience with the only light relief provided by the meeting – halfway – with the civilian policeman on duty there. Due to the number of Wrens, fortunately, this duty did not happen too often".

Later we seem to have been divided between Walton Rectory and Wavendon Park Farm. One ex-Wren describes the Abbey as 'freezing' and the Farm as 'heaven' – it was, in spite of baby frogs coming into our cabins en masse. The officer-in-Charge was ideal – firm but friendly.

I will try to create some picture of our work from the many and varied replies I have received in the space of two months. On the whole we worked two shifts (WRNS 'watches') from 8 am to 6 pm or 4 pm to midnight. A few mention doing night shift as well. We were transported to and from Bletchley Park mainly by 'hired' buses. A few people worked in the Naval Section in Hut 8 early on, and at some point the Japanese Section started off with a team of only four. In September 1942 the Section moved from Elmer's School to new building in the park proper, and in the following February it moved again to Hut 7, where Dr. Hugh Fosse was in charge – a brilliant and kindly man. Leslie Yoxall was largely responsible for the Naval Machine JN157, later known as JADE. (Bletchley Park Trust have an article on JADE written by Leslie Yoxall).

Several of the Wrens remembered working (often very hard) on this machine, and there was a sense of achievement and good natured rivalry with the opposite shift when they found their decrypts were working, by recognising a few Japanese words. Most of us did a one months course in the Japanese language – enough to recognise a message was not totally garbled. Others, mostly Foreign Office Staff, did a six month course. Here I quote;

"I helped to translate a captured book of call-signs".

"For six months I tried to learn to read and write Japanese (but not speak it – that was a different course for would-be interpreters of prisoners-of-war). Our instructor was John Owen Lloyd who had been Vice-Consul Tokyo 1937-41 and later Consul-General Osaka 1963-67"

A good message went straight to the translators, wherever they were based: we did not know. Quite a number of Wrens often worked with, or for, Foreign Office Staff, who were busy mainly with number codes. Quote from a F.O. staff member,

"I have memories of the great Hollerith machines that churned reams of groups of figures. This gave me courage to acquire an early Amstrad which I used to analyse 889 questionnaires to people who had a relative with Schizophrenia, this showed up some interesting correlations!"

One who went on to become a Professor of Mathematics remembers working exclusively on 'Subtractors' and several of us remember doing some of the 'spade work'. I can even recall the numbers in one subtractor – my family think this is why I retain the ability to remember telephone numbers.

One ex-Wren remembers an amazing amount about her work. – quote;

"I remember long hours of differencing – first of all trying to find the beginning of the message (the group for Begin message here – B.M.H.) which might be anywhere in the length of the message or traffic as we used to call it. On Friday afternoons we used to get the Dotteries up to date. Only in later days did we have the benefit of properly reproduced copies of Dotteries with the more frequent groups being marked with a square to signify their frequencies".

There is much on this subject and I am sure it can be available to anyone especially interested. A number of Wrens and Foreign Office staff were posted to Ceylon in 1944 to continue Japanese decoding. I know that there have been several small reunions. One ex-Wren had produced an article for her local British Legion branch about her time in Colombo – (Margaret says there are copies available). She continues; "The general impression I have of memories of our work is that most of us enjoyed it, a few were bored and everyone felt it was a good experience. One very good friend admits that she took to washing the Hut windows in moments of idleness!

The third thing I asked people about was their leisure time and that proved fascinating and often very amusing. Cycling, walking, reading and letter-writing figure largely. Here I quote again; firstly the Foreign Office staff:

"The BBC Symphony Orchestra was based in Bedford and that was great fun".

"I can remember attending a couple of 'Reviews' which enlivened the Christmas period."

Other shows took place in the Assembly Hall just outside the gates of the Park. Then there were:

"Lunchtime Scottish Country Dancing sessions organised by Hugh Fosse...very enjoyable and a break from routine." Many people refer happily to these dancing sessions.

The Wrens were, by the sound of things, more adventurous, I think due to the fact that we all lived together and had the opportunity to dream up ideas! We were invited to RAF and USAF dances at their Air bases nearby. These affairs were very popular as transport was laid on, but the best part was the American food! We also gave dances in the "Wrenneries" and I can remember the Officers going out round the bushes with their torches! A few more quotes;

"I met my husband at a Halloween Dance at Walton Rectory on 30.10.45."

"We tried 'messing about in boats' on the river at Bedford... the boats hired from BIFFEN, BASHAM and CHEETHAM! Truly."

"The monthly weekend leave sent us further affield, east, west, or north , or hitch-hiking to London where one could get a free ticket sent for the forces, from a kiosk in Trafalgar Square...if one was lucky!"

"One memorable weekend we hitch-hiked to London, and back, went to a matinee, a dance in the evening, stayed overnight in a hostel and had our meals in the British Restaurant in Leicester Square...all for 11 shillings and 8 pence each!

"On a day off we invariably hitched a lift to St. Albans, where we were able to exchange a pyjama chit for dress material at Green's

Drapery Store."

Rose's Store in Bedford was equally accommodating.

"I remember going to Whipsnade Zoo and running on Dunstable Downs like children on a day out!"

"I was on duty at Bletchley Park on VE-Day but I did have VJ-Day off"

Many of us were off that day and reached London somehow or other to join the enormous crowds outside Buckingham Palace. We cheered extra loudly when the Royal Family appeared on the balcony again and again.

All of us who worked in Hut 7 will agree that we made some dear and lifelong friends. It was a privilege to work in Hut 7 and nearly everyone feels that our experiences were beneficial.

Names of some of the Wrens in the Japanese Section

Merrie Acton (nee England)	Pam Adams (nee Dryland)
Edith Becker (nee Bennett)	Bunny Borland
Betty Everest (nee Ives)	Brenda Kelly (nee Curtis)
Beryl Middleton (nee Leigh)	Beryl Minter (nee Damen)
Ruth Perry (nee Roberts)	Eunice Phillips (nee Howard)
Margaret Picken	Winifred Pitt (nee Saunderson)
Joan Stevens (nee Balch)	Doris Watson (nee Hunt)
Belle Watson (nee Branfoot)	

KAY PICKETT (nee HARRISON)

I lived on a farm in West (now North) Yorkshire, with my parents and two younger sisters and was a schoolgirl when the war began. I had two uncles who were in the army – both serving in the dessert in the North African campaign. One was badly wounded and I think it was that happening which triggered my desire to do something positive to contribute towards the war effort – plus the fact that my love of England and its beautiful countryside made me feel passionate about it not becoming part of Hitler's conquests – which was a very real possibility in those dark days of the early forties. Thus it was in early 1944, when I was just eighteen, that I found myself as a probationary Wren at Wesley College in Leeds – and not too far from home. During those two weeks of squad drill, learning Naval terms, cleaning loos and experiencing that sort of camaraderie which exemplified subsequent life in the WRNS I had no real idea of what was to follow.

When at the end of the two weeks, the call came to report to

Chief Officer to find out what our category would be, there were three of us left, who had not been informed. As we had been overlooked until last – we began to think we had perhaps failed in some way to achieve the 'required' standard – whatever that may be, and resigned ourselves to getting our orders to go. However, we were called individually and I learnt I had been posted to HMS Pembroke V – and that it was a 'stone frigate' in Bucks; that the work I would do could only be revealed when I got there and, after being issued with rail tickets, etc. the journey was made. My memories of that first initiation to B.P. are somewhat hazy now. Certainly there was a great air of mystery about the place, as well as a great feeling that something vitally important was going on there. Of course secrecy was paramount.

My first quarters for three months, was Wavendon House – a rather imposing mansion, though as I remember it, I slept in what had been the stables with seemingly dozens of others – all in double bunks. I also have memories of sitting near the lake on lovely sunny days and being reluctant, on such days, when it was time to leave for evening watch. One never discussed work with any other Wren off duty, so one never had a complete picture of what was happening at work – only what went on in one's own section. Later on I would be quartered at Stockgrove Park – a modern mansion near Leighton Buzzard which was situated in quite beautiful grounds and parkland with a scenic lake and boathouse. Many a long walk have I enjoyed round those acres with or without fellow Wren-friends – very often in deep discussion on some heady subject – but never work!

I was assigned to Japanese Naval Section, in Block A. We were quite a small team of Wrens, amongst whom I remember Joan Unwin, Suzanne Lavy, Sylvia Purser, Janet Clark and Gwen Roberts and civilians Elizabeth Prince and Elizabeth Wyndham. Amongst the luminaries for whom we worked were Angus Wilson, Jack Plumb, Bentley Bridwater, Willie Ewing, Peter Laslett and John Beaumont. There were times of intense work when tensions ran high, when codes changed. At all times though we were a close-bonded and friendly group. Angus was particularly kind and considerate to his Wrens and I visited him several times after the war, when he lived in London, before my husband and I went to live in East Africa. Jack Plumb went on to an academic career at Cambridge University, Peter Laslett had some important career with

Radio 3, I believe, and I think most of the others pursued academic careers.

When not on watch our other pursuits seemed to consist of long cycle rides; trips to London, Bedford and Northampton (where I often went to see a boyfriend from my home town, – by now a member of the Repertory Theatre there). It was on a shopping spree to London that a Wren friend and I, coming out of Bond St. tube station, were carried back down the steps on a cushion of air as a V2 fell on John Lewis in Oxford Street. Concerts at the Albert Hall, theatre visits (at amazingly reasonable rates for service people – a certain number of reservations kept for them at every performance) – dances at RAF Cardington and American Air Corps. at Kimbolton and Bovindon: Concerts in the Bedford Corn Exchange and a never-to-be-forgotten dance when Glenn Miller and his band played. I can remember hearing endless renderings of Bing Crosby singing "Don't Fence Me In" night after night on evening watch, from one of the huts behind Block A.

I met my husband at B.P. He was one of the Japanese course 'subbies' with Capt. Tucker's course in Bedford and he worked in Block B – also Japanese Naval Section. There were several romances leading to marriage – Ishbel Ferguson married Clare – a dashing American from a nearby Air Corps. base, and another Wren, Sybil Wightman also married during her time there. Others, myself included, met our future husbands there and married after the war – in our case 1948.

When VE-Day came, and because it was expected, most of the personnel were allowed off on leave, with only a "skeleton" staff left on duty. For me it was a busy period – I helped another Wren, Joan Davis, organise a concert to celebrate the occasion at Stockgrove Park, and was on duty when the signal of capitulation came through from Grand Admiral Doenitz. But perhaps the highlight of this time was when I, along with other Wrens, joined an all-service choir which went to RAF Cardington, and briefly rehearsed by Leslie Woodgate, sang immediately after the first peace time broadcast by Mr Churchill. This was a poignant and momentous occasion. I still have our programme – amongst many other souvenirs and memorabilia which I collected together during my time as a Wren. Two hymns we sang – "Praise my Soul, the King Heaven", and "All People that on Earth do Dwell." Dr Welche, a Chaplain, conducted the service.

WE KEPT THE SECRET

Although my time at Bletchley Park was relatively short – it seems in retrospect so much longer, and, of course, when so much more has since been learnt (and still being discovered) of what happened there, and the importance of the work done there in the final scheme of the war, it makes it all so much more a major happening in the lives of all of us who were there. The interesting people one met and the lasting friendships made, are a testament to that incredible time – and the place where it happened.

CHAPTER 6

EASTCOTE AND STANMORE

MARGARET E. FRANCIS.

Margaret was a Wren from November 1943 – June 1945.

"I have very fond memories of my 'life in Pembroke V'. The friends I had made at Mill Hill, Mary Doole, Beryl Taylor and Sheila Saxton all decided we would volunteer for PV, not knowing what it was, but willing to take a chance that it would be interesting.

We left Mill Hill in a coach to go to Eastcote for training. Although we had been told to send our civilian clothing home one of our group had not done so and arrived at the coach with a mass of luggage. When we asked her why she had not sent some of her belongings home, she replied, "My dear, I thought we would have a porter to help us!". So much for life in the WRNS.

When we arrived at Eastcote, the officer who was assigned to train us was away for the weekend and would not be back until Monday, we had arrived on Friday, so , of course, we were put to work cleaning the billet. First of all we had to put up our own bunks and as the four of us all wanted an upper bunk we put up four bunks. During the night one collapsed, but luckily no-one was hurt. We four were assigned to clean the windows with just water and a cloth and we were expected to remove the paint still adhering to the windows. Luckily we got hold of some razor blades and did a creditable job.

When the officer arrived to start training us, she first asked our names. When I said my name was Margaret Francis, she said, "I'll remember you, you look like a Francis!" I thought that was very strange as Francis was my married name and I had only been married for eighteen months, but unfortunately she did remember me, and as I had a 'pageboy' hairdo, she was constantly on me to get it cut. Finally I had to put it up when I was anywhere near her and and on parade and that satisfied her.

We were very excited when we discovered we would be decoding and soon learned all the intricacies of the Bombe.

While at Eastcote I lost my liberty pass and P.O Bernstein, who knew me, gave me a very bad time. She told me if I were a sailor I could be put in irons for losing my liberty pass, etc. etc. I picked up my bag and started to walk out. She said, "Where are you going?" I said "If you are not going to let me in I'm going home." She let me in!

We were actually asked where we would like to go and the four of us opted for Gayhurst. We were lucky to all get the assignments we had requested. It was a lovely old manor house just a few miles from Newport Pagnell, and we were assigned to D watch and put in the guard room. We settled in very well. Our room mates were very compatible and I don't ever remember having any discord at all.

We worked in a bungalow a short distance away from the house with both Army and Navy code breaking machines. We had three watches, 8-4, 4-midnight, and midnight to 8 am. After the 8-4 watch we had 24 hours off duty, after the 4-midnight watch we had a two day stand off and after midnight to 8 am we came off at 8 am , went back for the 4-midnight shift, then had a five day stand off. We were allowed a pass to go home for the five days.

One thing about Gayhurst was we really didn't know we were in the service. We did not have to clean our own room, only make our beds and change the linen once a week. We sent our clothes to the laundry. We did no squad drill, we were given the choice of squad drill after a day watch or taking laundry from the van to the storage room. We opted for the laundry duty and only had to do it once a month.

The job, of course, was very demanding and if we ever missed a "job up" we were threatened with dire results. Fortunately I never found out about this as I never missed a "job up". I don't remember having too much trouble with keeping the secret. I knew it was vital not to tell, and was always very vague when anyone questioned me.

The 4-midnight watch was our favourite, because in the morning we could go horseback riding, have lunch at a lovely little inn, return to Gayhurst, have a bath and go on duty. Our least favourite was the midnight to 8 am watch. I remember my eyes feeling so tired when I was trying to check the drums for shorts in the brushes. It was always a relief when the "job up" was called on your machine and you could relax for a little while until a new menu arrived for you to set up on the machine.

We were taken on tour of Bletchley Park so that we could see what happened when we called in a possible code match, and were often given pep talks telling us what benefit had resulted from jobs we had brought up.

We had RAF maintenance men and one male Petty Officer – they did not live in the manor but in a cottage by the lake. We had excellent rapport with them all. The teamwork, now I look back, was extraordinary. We all worked together without any discord at all.

Sheila Saxton, Beryl Taylor, Margaret Francis, Mary Doole

WE KEPT THE SECRET

I remember just before D-Day the Second Officer put up a notice stating that "all Wren's clothing will be held up until the Navy's needs are satisfied." Referring of course to the stores. We all laughed so loud that she came out of her office, read the note and hastily removed it.

Mary Doole and I put in for a transfer. We thought we would like to break the Japanese code for a change. Second Officer Zuppinger came to talk to us about this just a few days after D-Day, telling us how unpatriotic we were to be requesting a transfer at this time. We explained that we had no idea D-Day was about to happen. We were turned down for our transfer.

At the end of the European War, we were given soldering irons and had to disconnect the machines, screw by screw. I think it is a pity that not one was left to be put in a museum."

BOBS BROOKE-TAYLOR (nee KIRBY)

I had been hoping to join the WRNS since I left boarding school in the March of 1943 so I was delighted to be called to Mill Hill in the November and looking forward to sea, ships and sailors!!

Eastcote was a quite a challenge for me in many ways; starting on arrival when we had to construct our own double bunks from a pile of metal and some spanners. It took me some weeks to get used to the timing of watches and the pattern of having to look after myself. I had never done my own washing and found learning to starch collars was a nightmare.

Since 1940 I had lived during school holidays with a maiden aunt, together with my brother who was only 12 in 1943. I had to try and see him during his school holidays and once a kind friend who lived at Eastcote asked him to stay so that I could take him in to London on a free day. We went to the Zoo!

As a member of 'D' watch 'Fire Team' we had our first practice using a small trailer. It was not small enough to fit through the gates across the public footpath and the practice was curtailed. I don't remember any other fire drills!

I used to go to London to dance at the Overseas League, to various musical concerts and later to Queens Ice Skating Club. I remember walking to Northolt (about 4 miles?) to see the RAF Pantomime "Cinderafella", and the long walk back afterwards – probably Christmas 1943.

On one occasion I was walking through Hyde Park when a V2

missile landed in Bayswater and the cloud of dust and smoke was amazing. From Eastcote we could sometimes see the glow and hear them landing in the East End, probably 15-20 miles away.

I had been involved with drama at school and I remember we had a few playreadings. In June 1944 I produced a play "The Young Person in Pink". I have no records of it as the local papers were full of D-Day reports that week. However, I do remember an uncomfortable ride in the back of a small van when I was taken to Denham Film Studios to choose furniture for the stage setting. I was in the chorus of the Revue which was produced after the War in Europe ended. At the time we were dismantling the Bombes and reducing them to their smallest components.

I had never been a very efficient operator, mostly because my hands were not big enough, and they hurt, and I did not enjoy the work, and we were firmly told that there would be no hope of promotion, and there was no possibility of moving to another outstation!

In June 1945 St. Hughes College, Oxford allowed me to sit for a delayed entrance exam. Third Officer Jelf kindly wrote a reference for me but, probably as I had read very little for 20 months, I was not successful. Instead I became a Paywriter and had a year at Harwich. I often worked seven days a week but I didn't mind – at least there was the sea, the ships and...the SAILORS!!!

MARY MOORE (nee DAVIS)

Mary from Newbury, Berks joined the WRNS in November 1943.

"Initial training was at Mill Hill for two weeks. This was time spent learning Naval ways and customs including how to salute and squad drill, there were few jobs available at this time for Wrens straight from school except as cooks, stewards or special duties. During interview it was emphasised that one was very suitable for special duties although the nature of the work was completely secret so no information could be given as to the work one was expected to do. As a nearly 18 year old how could one resist not finding out about this secret. The other girls who were going into this category seemed a friendly bunch and we all had good school certificate results and one had a degree.

We were kitted out with our uniform and posted to a place called Eastcote. This we discovered was in Middlesex on the Picadilly tube line just beyond Harrow. We wouldn't see the sea but we were very near London. On arrival we were shown into a large empty cabin, part of a very large single story building recently built. In the corners of each bay in this cabin was a pile of black metal and with the help of nuts, bolts and spanners we erected bunks and could then collect mattresses and bedding and make up our bunks.

Where we lived was the Quarters buildings and we were soon taken to another quite separate building across a lane, called Block B. We worked a watch system 8 am – 4 pm, 4 pm – midnight or midnight – 8 am changing each week and after night watch had 4 days leave. We found we were to operate machines called Bombes which were used to try and break into the German codes. Bombes have been described elsewhere. We found the work quite boring, there was a period of activity when a job was being set up and a need to be observant and make sure the plug board and drums had been set up correctly. Once the Bombe was running there could be hours of inactivity, unless there was a stop which when checked was useful and the magic message came back from Bletchley "job up". With up to 8 Bombes working at one time in a bay, the noise level was very high, but it was easy enough to talk to other Wrens and to the RAF chaps who kept our machines running. B Block had a very distinctive smell of warm oil, some Wrens disliked the work and some found handling the drums difficult because they had small hands, but most of us got on with it without complaint. We had a great deal of fun when off duty, the London theatres sent us free tickets for shows, after night watch we played dangerous but very energetic games of mixed hockey with the RAF.

When the war with Germany ended in 1945 our job was over, we sat outside B Block in lovely weather unscrewing brushes from drums, helping dismantle the Bombes. Eventually most of us were sent to other jobs elsewhere until our demob number came up. Our time at Eastcote had been a very strange period in our young lives but we had made some very good friends, felt we did contribute something to help the war effort and since all the information about Bletchley and Enigma has been out in the open it has given us an enormous amount of pride and pleasure that we accepted the offer to join special duties when we joined the WRNS."

Being a time of rationing and shortages, the subject of food often occupied our thoughts. Mary adds, "I remember on night watch we used to discuss what we would like to eat 'after the war'. I was longing for fresh peaches and bourbon biscuits (when I finally got some they were a terrible disappointment – (presumably ones taste buds alter with age). After this discussion we would go over to Quarters for mid-watch snack, 3-4am and all I can remember is Grade III (pale pink) salmon sandwiches and cups of nasty tea or coffee – virtually thrown at us by a disgruntled steward – losing her sleep and banished to Eastcote for misbehaving where there were sailors available!!"

Joining the WRNS brought young women into contact from many social groups. Mary mentions a "fascinating few days" when the daughter of a Duke joined their watch prior to her wedding to the son of a Marquis. They heard how an Aunt gave her emeralds when she was collecting emeralds!! They also heard how the bridegroom's batman was teaching the bride-to-be some domestic tasks, including how to shell peas. As Mary says, "an amazing glimpse into another world for most of us!"

ROSEMARY PODD (nee WILLIAMS)
Rosemary wrote of her memories in the WREN Magazine in October 1999.

"I joined the WRNS in May 1944 as soon as the lists opened after I left school. After the fortnight initial training at Mill Hill I was sent to Chelsea Polytechnic to train as a Radar Mechanic. Unfortunately, due to several bouts of tonsilitis (probably because I was used to the country air) I fell so far behind in my studies that I had to be transferred to another category. However, I did become quite adept at soldering!

In August 1944, I was posted to PV (HMS Pembroke V) at Eastcote, a sub station of Bletchley Park and I am very proud of my war service there. We learnt our craft on the job and worked eight hour shifts around the clock, one shift in the Bombe Bay and the other on a smaller machine in a side room. By intent I have little memory of what we did. Since we were bound by the Secrets Act for about thirty years it was better that way. We had RAF personnel to undertake the maintenance of the machines and to do any heavy lifting and there was also a bay manned by the Americans. We lived and worked in Nissen huts, the Quarters and the work area separated by a lane. During the winter of 1944 we had no heating for six weeks and were allowed to wear anything we liked to keep warm. I can also well remember having to attend

Divisions after night duty and standing outside in the bitter cold just longing to get to bed.

I remember we had to do duties in the galley and the horrible wooden sinks with a long channel underneath to take away the greasy water. The smell was not pleasant! Some of us spent time in sick bay with food poisoning which was not surprising!

We were not allowed to go in a pub within a twelve mile radius – one Wren was caught and was sentenced to six weeks confined to barracks and put on general duties. As my home was only five miles away from Eastcote (Rickmansworth) I used to take my friends home for the four days stand-off, which they enjoyed as many could only go home on long leaves and they enjoyed the home comforts – my parents were most hospitable. It was good to have a bath behind a locked door! Clean sheets could be a luxury too – we had no clean ones for six weeks once as the laundry service broke down – no hot water in a big freeze.

After the war in Europe ended our machines were of no use for breaking Japanese codes and had to be dismantled. We used to sit outside in glorious sunshine at long tables to do this task.

The job done I was transferred to HMS Drake as a Pay Writer with no training whatsoever and thrown into the deep end to work in the Petty Officers' Pay Section, on the fair ledger. My oppo taught me all I needed to know on that section. One day I had to take some papers to the Lt. Commander in Charge who greeted me by saying "So you are one of my intelligent Wrens". I have often wondered if he knew what we had been doing or was it because we had joined the section without any training? Needless to say, I didn't answer.

I was demobbed at the end of 1946. I wish I could have stayed in long enough to fulfil my ambition to become a Petty Officer and wear a tricorn hat!"

Rosemary has other recollections of her time at Eastcote e.g. "seeing the horrific pictures of Belson and other concentration camps posted on the notice boards after they were discovered, and going up to Buckingham Palace to see the King and Queen, the Princesses and Churchill on the balcony on VE-night. The excitement and thrill of being in the surge of all those happy and jubilant crowds and shouting "We want the King" over and over again." Rosemary mentions the difficulty of keeping the work secret, "I think we just said we were on special duties when asked".

RITA JENNER (nee COWLEY)

Rita lived in Walsall, Staffordshire and volunteered to serve in the WRNS. In 1943 she was told to report to Ballock, Scotland for training and did the usual amount of scrubbing etc. which few of us were used to. She had two exams before she was called for interview with a Wren Officer when she was told she would be sent to do work of a secret nature in London, but the Officer could give her no idea of the work entailed. Rita seems to have moved around more than most of us, as she was first sent to Mill Hill, then to Stanmore where she was trained on the Bombe machines then again off to Eastcote.

During her time at Eastcote she was issued with a pass up to 10.30 pm. She found her way to London where she had never been before, "it was so vast and daunting", she said. "I caught the tube back to Eastcote, as I thought, but I was on the District Line! Of course I arrived back late at Quarters and had to report to the Officer in the morning. I was 'torn off a strip' but thank goodness she believed me. I was a 'rookie'. Other Wrens said to me, "Next time you are late climb through a window we leave open." I assure you I was never late again!"

"At Eastcote the Bombes were so noisy and very hot work. I was just settling down when I moved again to Bletchley Park, Hut 11. I remember arriving at Bletchley Park and seeing the grand mansion, and some peculiar people. I thought to myself do I look the same to them?! I was quartered at Wavendon House. When I arrived there I saw a Wren come out of the stable. She had a lovely golden retriever with her. I learnt later that a Bombe was installed in there. The grounds were gorgeous, magnolia trees were in flower. The drive was so long from the lane I began to wonder what would be at the end. I wasn't disappointed."

"My stay in Hut 11 was short and I was moved to Hut 6. I met Ellen Spark, Irene Rimmer, Pam Bacon and Margaret Brannaghen. I was always happy at Bletchley and Wavendon House." Rita also mentions going to the cafe in Woburn Sands in their off duty times.

"I remember being on duty at midnight – 8.00 hours when someone came into our section and told us that one of the messages we had sorted meant one of the German large battleships had been sunk. We drank a toast in tea without milk to the event."

Rita describes their cabin at Wavendon House as being very

roomy. But they found it very difficult to sleep as everyone was doing different duties. "Being young was an asset. At Wavendon on Hallowe'en night we held a party in our cabin. My mother sent a fruit cake. Someone else supplied wine and the fire was lit. I can't remember what we used for a pumpkin. We all decided to ask our Quarters Officer to the party. She came. We were breaking regulations having the fire, also we could be confined to Quarters, but she relented and a good time was had by all. After the party we sat round a table with our glasses upside down. Someone asked whom would be a Prime Minister one day. The answer came, Anthony Eden!! I have never played the game since."

Rita says she cannot remember much about the work "as it was drummed into us to keep it secret. I was always being asked which category I was in. On answering 'Writer', they said but you have no 'W' on your arm.

(We in Special Duties had no badge at all until we were made a Leading Wren and were given a badge of rank, but no badge to show our Special Duties category, which did make life difficult when meeting other service personnel. G.P.)

Rita mentions hitch-hiking to Luton or Leighton Buzzard and going to shops there who exchanged pyjama chitties for material. "We came back one day for duty at 1600 – midnight on a trailer the RAF used for transporting aircraft. When we arrived at B.P. gates, we looked like scarecrows!" She adds, "we worked hard and had fun. I remember going to the American dances where the food was super. I also remember going to the cinema in Bletchley which was called the Flea Pit, but I never caught any. One frightening aspect I remember, was walking through the lanes at night when a buzz bomb flew over. I would pray 'please God don't let the engine cut out, let it fly on."

"My parents came to stay at one of the cottages in Woburn Sands and my American boyfriend asked my father if he could marry me. My father said, "You must ask Rita herself." But I said 'No'.

Rita bought a utility bike and says, "It was hard to ride, but worth it."

(with the lack of transport in those times it was often shank's pony (walking), so a bicycle was a great asset in those long lanes around our quarters. G.P.)

Rita adds "My friend Jean Cowl, who worked in the Jap Section and lived at Woburn Abbey, went to Colombo, but caught Malaria.

We lost contact after being demobbed."

KAY ROE (nee MAKINSON)

Most of my memories are of Eastcote, although after VE-day I was transferred to Bletchley and quartered at Wavendon House in the stables where we had a hornet's nest over the door.

At Eastcote I remember going across to the galley in the early hours of the morning for our break and getting some bread and marg, with little oven beetles squashed between the plates. I also remember the summer of 1944 being hot and we came off watch at 8 am and sat around the cabins. I had washed my hair and it was drying in the sun. One by one the girls must have gone to bed and I must have fallen asleep. I wakened in the afternoon with swollen lids and a splitting headache. Someone said that sunstroke was an offence in the Navy, so being only 18 years old and having been subject to strict discipline all my life (as we were), I worked on , in terrible distress with a peeling face and pounding head – but I have never sat in the sun since!

My happiest memories are when we used to go up to London to the 'Stagedoor Canteen', 'Nuffield Centre' etc. and every Tuesday (shifts permitting) we sat watching Glen Miller (I think it was the Queensbury Club) conduct the American Forces Band (AEF) which was broadcast. He smiled at my friend (Ann Parkinson) and after the show we got his autograph! I also remember being on the Underground Station (just after arriving). I said, 'Oh look there is a plane on fire!' It cut out, and everybody got down and we just stood there like idiots, because nobody had thought to tell us about the 'Buzz-bombs' (Doodle-bugs or V1s).

I spent most of my working time in one particular bay and as you came out and crossed the corridor, there opposite were our toilets. One night they suddenly transferred me to another bay. As I came out of the toilet I found it was the mens!

ROMA DAVIES (nee STENNING)

The criteria for the job was to be at least 5' 6" tall, have matric in Maths and be a bit mechanically minded...so there I was at the age of 17 1/2 wondering just what PV meant – very soon I was told and before long was signing the Official Secrets Act. It was at the beginning of 1945 I had come straight from boarding school into the WRNS and to Eastcote. I was working on these huge machines – underground – and mostly on duty at night. I was only aware of my own part in all of this, I had no idea of the overall picture and no notion of what my friends were doing. Here we were working on this vital project for the princely sum of nine shillings a week, and on that we took ourselves out for suppers, the cinema and even trips to the West End to the Variety Club.

I only saw the sea and ships when I went home to Plymouth – of course by now the city (Plymouth) was completely flattened but we in London were having to contend with the V Bombs which were equally frightening.

After a few months the European war was over – I joined the many thousands of folk outside Buckingham Palace on VE-Day and then back to base, we demolished every bit of evidence of our ever being there. These colossal machines were rendered to minute pieces – loaded on to lorries and all papers destroyed. We were sent on to Stanmore and helped there with the same exercise and now on to Bletchley Park. This was all very different. I had very splendid accommodation in Wavendon House. The bedroom for two of us was not very big but did house an extremely large floor to ceiling dark wood wardrobe with one section which had little pull out drawers on the front of which had plaques saying 'ties, collars, handkerchieves, shirts...etc.' I had never seen such things other than in shops. I was impressed with the very ornate bathroom which boasted an enormous gilded mirror covering the wall over the bath. There was a minstrals gallery running round the landing with a sweeping staircase, but we had to use the back stairs!

One evening we were told we had to attend a compulsory lecture on 'Home Affairs' – how boring we all thought and took with us books, sewing and knitting, but what a mistake and how wrong we were to prejudge the talk – the speaker was Constance Spry and she was quite spell-binding. I remember her as a little woman wearing masses of silver bracelets which jingled as she waved her arms telling us of her world of flower arranging. I was enthralled – so much so I have been fascinated with the subject ever since and have been a member of NAFAS for thirty years raising thousands of pounds for charity with flowers. Of course I have the beautiful rose called Constance Spry in my garden.

I worked on the Japanese desk at B.P and sat next to one of our very well known authors of today – not only did she show me the ropes but taught me some very naughty rugger songs. I have often laughed since and would doubt if she would want to remember that bit!

One of the Naval Dental Surgeons looked to me to be very like Gregory Peck (a favourite film star of mine at the time) and I bravely let him give me four particularly large fillings at the back of my mouth and I still have proof of that experience to this day. I can well remember the General Election of 1945 being a very sobering affair as several of my friends' fathers were suddenly in the news losing positions in Government and the Civil Service.

By now Wrens were needed in Ceylon and I volunteered. My father sent a telegram to the Admiralty giving his consent for me to go, but in fact I was not allowed to as I was still under 18, and when the Japanese war was over I was transferred to Supply. After a short spell at Skegness, it was on to Corsham where, of course, Prince Phillip was stationed and we had all the excitement and more secrets to keep which were of his meetings locally with Princess Elizabeth.

Although all this was a very long time ago and a very serious time in our lives, I do have many happy memories and keep closely in touch with a wonderful friend made at Wavendon. I do so hope and trust they will eventually be able to restore Bletchley Park to somewhere near to what it was as a permanent reminder of the success of those years.

AUDREY WIND

I had to report for war service in the early summer of 1944 and asked to go into the WRNS. I was told that no more woman were being accepted in to the WRNS, but I persevered, quoting a strong family connection with the Royal Navy and was finally accepted. I was told to report to Tulliechewan Castle on the shores of Loch Lomond in Scotland, on August 16th for initial training.

Tulliechewan consisted of the castle on the hill, where the Officers lived, and a number of Nissen huts below, where we lived, together with a drill hall, a mess, a forecastle, galley and various offices, etc.

The WRNS was the only one of the three women's services which operated this initial training scheme. We had some pretty taxing jobs to do during this fortnight, such as cleaning out lavatories and incinerators, scrubbing the steps of the castle by the light of a torch at 7 am etc., to see what we were made of. During this time we had the option to leave (and do service elsewhere); likewise the WRNS had the option to tell us we were not suitable. I quite enjoyed this training period, and incidentally, had my first proper night's sleep at Tulliechewan after two years of bombing, doodle-bugs and shelling in Folkestone.

During the second week, six of us were told to report to the castle. We racked our brains to try and think what we had done wrong, but could think of nothing! When we arrived, we were told to sit outside a room in alphabetical order. I was number 5, since fortunately for me there was one called Wright. The first Pro-Wren was called in, and we waited with baited breath for her to come out and tell us what we were there for, but, when the door opened, she marched straight past us and out of the castle! This was repeated with each one until it was my turn. I marched into the room to find a long table, behind which were seated about half-a-dozen very important looking people, some in uniform, some in mufti. I stood to attention before them, and one – the WRNS Officer, I think – told me they wanted me to do some very secret work, but couldn't tell me what, and would I like to go away and think about it? I said I would do it, whatever it was, was thanked, and told that when I left the room, I must not mention anything at all about the matter to anyone. I was then told 'About turn' and I marched out of the room and straight past poor Pro-Wren Wright! I learned much later that my local Police had been contacted to check that I had a clean sheet and no subversive leanings!

Those of us who were selected were soon posted to the Wesley College at Headingly, Leeds, where we stayed for one week, and from there straight to Eastcote, one of the out-stations of Bletchley Park, the war-time Government Code and Cypher School – a title we were forbidden ever to utter. We were called Pembroke V (PV) Wrens on special duties X.

There were a thousand Wrens at Eastcote when I was there, 250 on each of the four watches, A, B, C and D. I was to join 'C' Watch. The premises – at the far end of Lime Grove – consisted of 'A' Block, where we all lived, and 'B' Block, the heavily guarded and fortified place where we worked. The eight cabins in 'A' Block, two to each watch, were named after Royal Naval Aircraft Carriers, and I was in HMS Formidable – a happy coincidence, since my cousin was serving as a Commander on HMS Formidable at that time. Each watch had an Officer and four Petty Officers. Since people hardly ever moved away, it was easy to see why we had been told that there was virtually no chance of promotion!

The people who looked after us in 'A' Block, including the Officer, had no idea what went on in 'B' Block, such was the level of security.

We were to learn the day after we arrived at Eastcote that we were to be involved in the work of trying to break the German Enigma Codes, and that we would be trained to operate the Bombes (named after the Polish 'Bomba') a large number of which were housed in 'B' Block at Eastcote. We were issued with special passes bearing our photographs, and although the men on guard at 'B' block got to know us, we always had to go through an identity procedure each time we entered. The Block had a very high wall all round it, and there was a good deal of barbed wire round about.

The huge rooms in 'B' Block, all branching off the main corridor were called bays, and each bay was named after a country. The machines in a particular bay were named after towns in that country. I worked mostly in Yugoslavia, on a Bombe called 'Split'. By each Bombe was a large table and a chair. There was a small room at the end of each bay where we went to test 'stops' on small machines, and where if it was a good 'stop', we sent the result over a scrambled line to Bletchley Park. One of the end bays was staffed by United States service personnel, and we also had members of the RAF working there, together with the Post Office engineers, who serviced the machines.

The detail of how we operated the Bombes has been very well documented by Diana Payne in chapter 17 of the book "Codebreakers", and so I will not repeat it here. All I will add is that in all branches of code-breaking, the work was often tedious, but the vital nature of it kept us alert at all times, even when we were very tired, which we often were, owing to the strain involved and the fact that we were working watches of an eight hour duration, a week of each watch. After night watch we had to attend Divisions, which was purgatory when all we wanted to do was to get to bed! After our week of night watch we had what was called a 'Friday While', which consisted of four days off. We had regular security lectures, when secrecy was re-emphasised, any lapses anywhere in the service referred to, and bits of successful code-breaking and its results reported.

Everyone in 'B' Block had his or her own mug, many of them elaborately painted, and a tea trolley would come round once on each watch. Sometime during the watch, we went over to 'A' Block for a meal, but these visits had to be staggered, so that the Bombes could be kept in operation. There was a public footpath between Blocks 'A' and 'B' and there had been reports of attacks, and so it was quite an ordeal to go across on one's own on night watch at about 3 or 4 am. I remember very well that I used to run across at something approaching Olympic speed on those occasions.

During my time at Eastcote, quite a good concert was put on one evening by people who were not on duty. Wren Audrey Pullen, who used to broadcast on BBC radio when duties permitted, took part, and there was quite a lot of other talent.

There was a very good W.V.S. canteen at Ruislip, a couple of stops away on the tube, and we used to go there as often as possible. A kindly husband and wife, who helped there, had 'open house' in their own home for about six of us, and shared their rations with us. I kept in touch with them until they died, as did another member of our group.

When on evening watch, it was possible to go into London on the tube for a few hours, and we sometimes went to Kew Gardens, where it was both tranquil and fairly safe from air raids. A friend and I managed to go to central London on VE-day, and we attended the morning service of thanksgiving in Westminster Abbey. We also had a marvellous view, standing on the large base of a lamp-post, of the King and Queen, Winston Churchhill, and many others, who drove through the streets past cheering crowds.

Towards the end of the war in Europe, we were told that Special Duties X Wrens would be needed to go to Colombo, and I volunteered for this, which I had to do since I was under-age for compulsory overseas service. I had my medical, but then the Atom Bombs on Hiroshima and Nagasaki brought the war with Japan to an end, and so none of us were sent there.

Although our Special Duties had come to an end, the WRNS refused to demobilise us, and we had to move to other categories – but that's another story!

RUTH BOURNE (nee HENRY)

When I was not quite eighteen. I exchanged my school uniform navy-blue knickers with a pocket in the leg, for a pair of similar ones called 'black-outs' which were an integral part of the uniform of the WRNS. Thus I made my transition from girlhood to womanhood and found myself travelling alone to Glasgow, part of the British Isles I had never been to before. At training camp in Tulliechewan I was overwhelmed by the variety of young women I had never met before. The fortnight I spent there was in fact a whirlwind of new experiences, but very exciting and also humbling.

I felt outraged at having to scrub lavatory floors until I discovered my co-cleaner had an Oxford degree but scrubbed away uncomplainingly; and by the time I had finished this baptism of fire, I had all my corners rubbed off, so was undismayed when after a long tiring journey to Eastcote, I had to walk that long long road to the Wrennery absolutely laden down with an issue kit-bag full of WRNS serge uniform as well as the civvies I started out with.

I think I was lucky to have experienced many years as an evacuee in North Wales, where I had been allocated attic rooms usually shared with a cistern which swished every time water was drawn. Otherwise I would have been alarmed at having to share a dormitory (cabin) with 71 other Wrens most of whom seemed to have arrived before me and were now occupying the upper bunks. In fact, the whole set up of dormitories, school food, noise, lack of privacy and endless rules, seemed to me no different from the days I had spent at a boarding school in Colwyn Bay where I had been temporarily dumped at the outset of war. So in many ways I went on being a schoolgirl until I settled down to the routine, and suddenly found myself in a completely new role.

Again for the FIRST TIME, I had the choice about what I could do during the free periods between the watches at Eastcote. On a day watch one had free time to go to cinemas, or any dances held in the building or outside by invitation to other Army camps or airfields. Evening watch gave freedom to explore local areas or go into London, the Big Smoke, and be offered the many 'freebies' and other welcome privileges offered to Service-people. And if you were able and willing to burn your candle at both ends, the night watch could be ended with a quick kip, followed by an afternoon and evening going to the theatre, dancing, having fun at the Stage Door Canteen – and other pleasurable escapades which I as a young newly-fledged woman, had not hitherto had any chance to enjoy.

I think what came about as a result of this experience was a very speedy maturation process. Personally, I learned very quickly to sum up people who presented themselves as "Here I am, as I am, take it or leave it". We came from unknown backgrounds, in uniform, nothing to give us clues about our socio-economic groups. I had to learn by trial and error, thrown into adult life at the deep end on a sink or swim basis.

I believe that having the Wren uniform did in some measure give me a protective covering as it were, because I found that this did command a certain respect from newly-met servicemen. Also having the amount of restraint afforded by the rules spoken and unspoken, regarding when we had to be back in Quarters, and about we had to behave in ways befitting to our uniforms, gave me and maybe others, safe boundaries from which we could operate.

I freely admit that I enjoyed being flirted with at socials, the cheeky banter with the technicians on watch, being asked "Can I kiss you goodnight?" at the gates-alas, how many young women today merit, or feel that they merit, such a choice or such consideration?

My predominant feelings during those two years in the Service were of quite wondrous excitement, tinged with just the right amount of trepidation needed for self-preservation during times of new adventure. Despite the hard work and difficult conditions, I wouldn't have missed it for the world.

Ruth was at Eastcote and Stanmore 1944-46.

She also writes of her revisit to Eastcote many years later. "On August 11th 1998 I went with a group down Memory Grove-Lime Grove, Eastcote to visit the site of one of the Bletchley Park out-stations where 120 Bombes were installed in long artificially lit Bombe bays.

We were four visitors: John Gallehawk who organised the tour, and who does sterling work at the Bletchley Park Museum as well as writing informative pamphlets which can be bought there; John Harper from the Computer Conservation Society who is collating information and working on the Bombe Rebuild project; Bernard Rafftery, the chief RAF engineer at Eastcote at the time in charge of the mechanics who were servicing the machines, and who was a mine of information; and myself. The bays in the high security building known as 'B' Block were named after Allied and occupied, nations, and each machine was named after a city or town in that country. Mr Rafftery remembered them all.

I was taken aback by the changes in Old HMS Pembroke V

Eastcote. 'B' Block which was once surrounded by high walls, blast proof and topped by barbed wire, with the entrance guarded by an armed Marine – all gone! The way it looks now it could be a Primary School, harmless, innocuous. Only a vestige of one wall behind the building. Open entry. And many windows everywhere, where there were once only thin, high, glazed slits to keep out prying eyes.

On entering I immediately noticed the carpeting in the corridors – as Bernard said, they did not appear as durable as those of 1943-45 which had concrete textured pile. I recognised 'my' bay, Norway, and spotted the hatch between the machine bay and the checking room which had been bricked in, but where the lintel still showed. The American Secretary who now works there was quite surprised and intrigued to learn of its original history. All the bays are now converted into American Offices, and we are told that in a few years all the building will be demolished to make way for a factory development.

As for the 'Wrennery', I well remembered the half-mile corridors with the cabins leading off on either side, named after battleships. I went into one of these seventy-two bedded dormitories and gazed at vast empty space littered with fluff and the odd bits of debris that seems to cover areas long unoccupied. As I closed my eyes I could see it all happening again; girls putting on their night creams, potions and lotions after the lights were out; giggling about exploits with officer types at the 'Blue Cockatoo' – the place to BE; some of the lucky ones fixing their pearls under their shirts because pearls lose their lustre if they're unworn. What a mixed crew we were! Forty of us sleeping down one side, thirty-two down the other, all in two-tiered bunks – and if the girl above you was a heavy mover, it was a rocky night for you mate! And what about the four day stand-off every month, before which the cabin had to be spit-and-polished, using black boot polish and 'Lord Nuffield's' (a packet a month donated free by himself and which otherwise were hard to get). Then the frantic scrub ourselves before presenting ourselves in spotless white shirts at Pay Parade (£2.10 a fortnight all found) before tearing down Lime Grove to catch the trains home for a rest and hopefully a bit of pampering, before re-starting the next months watches.

I walked past the foc'sle, now also a black floored empty space, recalling the dances we used to have with the RAF Mechanics without whom the noisy Bombes would not have been in action 24 hours a day. Those were fun times, and there were many because Eastcote was not that far from the West End of London and all it had to offer by the way of free tickets to shows, available from a booth in Leicester Square; or nights dancing away on the Covent Garden floor constructed above the stalls, where one could meet people from all over the world.

JENNY CONDUIT (nee DAVIES)
STANMORE

In 1942 I was seventeen and after a rather narrow middle-class childhood was contemplating with some excitement what part I would play in the war effort. Having discarded some ideas, I was floundering. When my mother and I went up to London and I saw a group of Wrens on the bus. I was transfixed with delight and knew that I wanted to be with them. Six months later and just eighteen I was in, and my family were grateful to see me depart because the poor things were bored to tears by my endless babbling about what I would do "When I am in the WRNS".

After a tough but friendly fortnight at Mill Hill training station about twenty of us were herded into a room and told that we had been selected to do this special and highly secret work and we had to decide now before we were told more. Rumours had reached us that the work was hard and boring but as I was completely unqualified for anything I thought I had better agree.

Instead of being sent to a Naval Station we were driven just a few miles to Stanmore, Middlesex where we were housed in modern single storey buildings. After we had settled in we were taken to the block where we were to work. This area was surrounded by high walls and barbed wire and guarded by Royal Marines. Once inside we had to sign the Official Secrets Act then we were let in to the big secret. To this day it amazes me that young naive girls were privy to such knowledge and expected not to reveal it. In the beginning it was very hard, I thought I would burst with the enormity and excitement of such information, but as time went on and after constant training about security it became easier, in fact we found we were able to block out thoughts of the work once we were out of the building. We had to learn how to parry awkward questions from friends and family either with jokes or lies. When F.W Winterbotham's book "The Ultra Secret" was published in 1974 and the story exploded on television and in the newspapers I found that I was unable to stop chattering about it for days. All this knowledge with which I had expected to go to the grave came bubbling up to the surface. I still feel sad that my mother died before I was able to tell her.

The feeling of camaraderie amongst us was strong, we felt very close in our shared secret and I made many lasting friendships. From what I have read later, life at Stanmore was far more disciplined than at the smaller stations. We always seemed to be marching somewhere, having squad drill and kit inspections – just what we needed after a long night watch! The work we did on the Bombes has been described often, so I won't mention it except to say that we had to be reasonably tall and strong. It was unrewarding in that we never knew what we had achieved but we were always delighted when we heard the words "Jobs up" because we then knew that the message had been decoded and that was our purpose. I notice now that the sub-stations are rarely or never mentioned which is a bit sad for us as there were about five hundred Wrens at Stanmore, even more at Eastcote and many RAF technicians. There is no doubt that it was a stressful job. The watchkeeping hours changed every week and played havoc with our digestions and sleeping habits. What it did to our social lives was dire, one met a nice young man one week and when he wanted to see you again, lo and behold it was the anti-social 4-12 watch. The food at Stanmore left much to be desired, having been at boarding school I wasn't fussy but I can still see the grisly pile of sad, burnt, cold and soggy slices of cheese on toast that we were expected to survive on in the small hours.

Stanmore was at the end of the Bakerloo line, so the West End was available to us and on our sleeping-out passes we would book into the YWCA which enabled us to stay out a bit later. Girls of our age today would not easily take to being back in Quarters by 10.30 pm and twice a week actually being allowed a late pass to 11.30 pm. We were usually able to get free theatre tickets from Forces Canteens or we went to the Queensbury Club or Nuffield Centre and saw many fine entertainers. Dancing was to be had in these clubs and at Covent Garden. Once a year each watch was allowed to hold a dance in Quarters and invitations were sent to various service establishments in the district. We were sent invitations too, these were put on the notice board and we added our names if we wanted to go. There was always great competition to get to the American parties, the hospitality was wonderful and we always came away having had gorgeous food and free cigarettes. On one memorable occasion when all our hosts were drunk and even the band collapsed, I heard our chaperoning Wren Officer telling the American Colonel that she didn't think we would be allowed to go there again, but he was too far gone himself to take it in!

The worst of the bombing in London was over but I remember quite a few bombs and then we had the unpleasant Doodle-bugs and rockets. Many is the time I have had to fling myself to the ground when the dreaded sound of the engine cutting out came, ruining my precious black silk stockings – a minor tragedy in those days of shortages and rationing. I don't think we realised the strain of the bombs until it was all over and the relief from fear felt so wonderful.

In 1945 the German War was over and suddenly we were redundant. Watchkeeping ceased and we were set to work dismantling the Bombes. I recall sitting at trestle tables unscrewing the drums. Gradually we were dispersed to other categories and I was drafted to Plymouth, a port at last! My job was helping to demobilise sailors and I worked in the R.N. Barracks, Davenport.

I had become very thin and tired after two and a half years watchkeeping, but after a few weeks in Plymouth with the sea air, much better food and regular hours I felt re-born and enjoyed my last year in the WRNS hugely and felt part of the Navy at last. All the time, despite the awful hours, poor food, hard discipline and dreary work we were sustained by the knowledge that what we were doing really mattered and was going to win the war – we were also young and free and enjoyed ourselves as much as we could.

ANNE FINDING (nee HOOD)

Anne was posted to Eastcote. Stanmore, Bletchley Park and back to Stanmore. She writes;

"The time was late December 1943 and I noticed a tiny item in The Times stating that recruitment for the WRNS would be suspended on 31 December for the time being. My first love had been killed at sea on an oil tanker in one of the Atlantic convoys and I was determined to join the Wrens, whatever the cost. With only enough money to get me to and from Bristol by bus I cycled from my father's vicarage to the nearest spot where I could leave my bicycle and catch the bus. Suffice it to say that I did not have an easy time finding the opportunity to join at any of the recruiting offices. The Royal Navy recruiting people were less than helpful, eventually someone on the RAF office suggested a place miles away from the centre. I had been walking all day with nothing to eat or drink inside me and late in the afternoon made it to the WRNS Depot where they took pity on me and a kind Wren Officer said she would make an exception and take my details. Arriving home in the cold damp evening I announced that I had indeed filled in the necessary papers. My mother (who did not wish me to join up) did not speak to me for a long time. My eighteenth birthday was in the January. I made it but had to stay at home until mid February as my mother was having a baby. The cold hungry walk of some 12+ miles in Bristol had been worth it.

Training at Mill Hill and then a ride in the back of a utility wagon. "Where am I going?" I asked. "You'll know when you get there", came the terse reply. End of subject. It was the beginning of March and Lime Grove, Eastcote, not the most prepossessing of spots and thus it all began. Many will know that part of it.

The secrecy of it all was sometimes the difficult part. One went home and people always knew somebody whose daughter was doing something important...'like plotting you know, in the Air Force' and so on. 'And what are you doing then?' or similar comments which I managed to ward off somehow.

One of the worst moments came when I was struck with a bad dose of influenza and needed a certificate from the medical officer at the nearby RAF camp. The chief Medical Officer was a family friend and, unfortunately, after several calls as I was getting anxious, my father ascertained that he was away for a week on a course and one of his colleagues would visit. This he did eventually, and ill though I was I knew immediately what to expect. In front of my father he asked me a few cursory questions, beginning with 'What's your name girl?'. An auspicious start, followed by 'What do you do?'. My father intervened saying that I was ill with influenza, which the doctor had diagnosed, anyway, and that I needed a certificate due to being unfit to travel. The conversation then took another turn:

M.O 'Why does she want a medical certificate, Padre?' – my

father was visiting certain gun-sites and balloon-sites in the area. My father replied that it was necessary.

M.O. 'Don't worry about it, Padre. These girls aren't important, they only fill in for the more menial jobs, you know cleaning, cooking, maybe something simple in the office, that kind of thing you know!'

My father by that time had had enough and said in a dangerously quiet voice 'Will you step outside, Doctor, now. I have something to say to you.' Somewhat unwillingly, the Medical officer left with my father, I caught my father saying 'I don't know exactly what my daughter does, but I think it is something about which she is not allowed to talk. I respect her unwillingness and would be grateful if you could give me the signed certificate so that I can send it to Stanmore for her'. My fathers voice was low, spoken in a tone which I knew boded ill for the recipient. The M.O. then said he had not bothered to bring any certificates, with the relevant material to hand he would see that it was sent to the right address. He took no further action and I was punished on return to Stanmore for not sending in the requisite certificate.

Later in the early 70s, a unique situation arose. I was running an international seminar in the then West Germany and was waylaid by a particularly obnoxious German Army Major who then piled in, in German as follows:

"You English think you won the war but I tell you one thing you never did, you never understood our wonderful Enigma machine. Our secrets were our secrets and we knew all yours." (Working in Germany for many years I found that the Brits were 'The English').

How I longed to respond with 'How little you know buddy, how little you know.' All I could do was smile and shrug my shoulders. C'est la vie!

AN EXPLANATION OF THE TURING BOMBE
by ANTHONY E. SALE F.B.C.S.

This device developed by Alan Turing and others at Bletchley Park, followed an original idea by Marian Rejewski, the famous Polish code breaker. It was devised in order to break the German Enigma cipher. This cipher used the Enigma machine to encipher messages which were then transmitted using Morse code.

The Enigma machine used three, later four, rotors or wheels in the machine to provide a continuously changing electrical path from an input key to an output lamp. The operator pressed down a key on the typewriter-like keyboard and a lamp lit, illuminating a letter on the panel behind the keyboard. This was the enciphered letter of the key just pressed and had to be written down for later transmission by Morse Code on a radio link. These enciphered messages could be intercepted using radio receivers listening to the Morse Code transmissions. However, intercepting was one thing, deciphering was quite another.

Enigma allowed an enormous number of different settings or start positions to be used for each message. The code breakers had to find which rotors were in the machine and in which order. Then the ringstellung or alphabet setting on each rotor used has to be found. The start position of each rotor had to be worked out and finally the plug board (stecker) connections had to be found. The total number of combinations of all these elements, for just a three rotor Enigma, is 150,000,000,000,000,000,000 or 1.5 times 10 to the power 20. The Turing Bombe tackled this vast complexity through the use of "cribs". In Bletchley Park jargon a crib was a section of German text which was thought, from other clues, to be the actual text enciphered to produce the intercepted Enigma cipher text. The Germans were particularly lax in their use of Enigma and left all sorts of clues around which allowed cribs to be identified.

When a crib had been identified for a particular message, a so-called menu was constructed with pencil and paper. This menu was formed from places in the crib where enciphered letters and crib letters formed patterns of relationships.

The menu was then plugged up on the Bombe by the WRNS operators. This involved selecting sets of rotors equivalent to those that might have been used for this enciphered message and then plugging up at the rear of the Bombe all the electrical connections corresponding to the menu relationships. The Bombe was then set running at high speed searching for rotor positions at which all the relationships were satisfied. If one was found then the Bombe stopped. This was known as a drop. This result then had to be tested to see if it actually deciphered the message. A complete run through all possible rotor positions took 15 minutes. There were 60 sets of rotors so a whole run on all rotor orders might take up to 30 hours

The power of the Bombe as a search engine was quite astounding. It was a highly parallel dedicated machine with electrical current flowing through many hundreds of wires at the same time giving a resolution of one position of the rotors on 10 millisecond, (10 thousandths of a second). A computer simulation of the Bombe running on a modern Pentium PC takes 18 hours to do what the Bombe did in 15 minutes.

The Turing Bombe

Turing realised that traffic analysis could be used to predict the text of some parts of the enciphered messages. The Bombe could then be used to test, at high speed, whether there were any possible settings of the rotor which translated the enciphered characters into the deduced characters. More importantly, using his mathematical skills, he showed that it was far quicker to prove that a transformation from ciphered to deduced text **precluded** a vast number of possible rotor combinations and starting positions

Welchman came across an idea known as the Diagonal Board which when attached to the Bombe increased its power significantly.

The Bombe

CHAPTER 7

'Y' SECTION WT AND DF OPERATORS

BETTY BROOK (nee BAKER)

On 17th April 1942, with much trepidation, I took the train from Waterloo to Droxford on the Watercress Line, en-route for Soberton Towers to join the WRNS.

My father decided to accompany me as far as Alton where we had to change. Having ascertained from peeking at the addresses on other girls' luggage that we were nearly all bound for the same place – he, although generally a shy man, managed to strike up conversation with the oldest and most sensible looking of the lot. By the time we had got to Alton he had made her promise him to keep an eye on me. We parted on Alton Station; me with a pocketful of loose change in case I needed to ring him up!

We arrived at Droxford Station and then walked to Soberton Towers I think, it was not far. On arriving and being ushered in, I was assigned to Drake Cabin, chose a bunk and promptly made friends with a girl in the next bed, having successfully dodged the trustworthy companion my father had picked for me.

For the next six months life revolved around learning how to take down Morse Code, and the basic principles of wireless telegraphy, interspersed – naturally – with time off when the nearest place of amusement drew us like a magnet (namely Pompey) where the real 'matelots' hung out. On being picked up by one, discovering he had been in the Navy for all of three months too! Having passed out as WT Operators we were all drafted to the WT Station at Scarborough, a rather ramshackle cramped building in Sandybed Lane. Here we were initiated into watch keeping, listening in on a German frequency, taking down the messages sent, and all the chit-chat between the stations that formed the group. If a message was preceded by the date alone with no serial number we knew at once it was sent by a ship, so we had to call out our frequency and the man on control would call it on the landline to all the DF stations who would then get a bearing on it. A very short message preceded by a sinister sounding E Bar was a U-Boat transmitting, and naturally had to be dealt with in double quick time by all concerned, usually successfully I might add.

A Warrent Officer, whose name escapes me, gave us a little pep talk when we first arrived, stressing the need for secrecy as we were listening to the Germans who were sending messages in the Enigma Code. He casually remarked almost as an after-thought that he had seen it, it was very nice, and that those messages had to be teleprinted to Bletchley within five minutes – where they were decoded by cryptographers, and to Washington within fifteen minutes. All this we found very intriguing but slightly mystifying. It became very repetitious and we soon became blasé about it, even after having pointed out to us in hushed whispers "the set that sunk the Bismark". Apparently the operator on it had called out the frequency when the Bismark had transmitted a message and the DF's had got a bearing on it, so leading to the discovery of its whereabouts. I would dearly love to have these facts verified just to prove to myself that I did not dream them. Even though, at the time I was probably more interested in going dancing at the Royal Hotel!

After a few weeks we all moved to the brand new station on the moors above Scarborough, which was much more spacious and airy even though it was underground. When visiting Scarborough on a reunion a few years ago, we were pointed it out by the current station commander, from the car park I might add as we were not allowed on the site. Alas our brand new station is now derelict.

After about a year of watch-keeping at WT station I, in the company of a few others, was sent to the local DF (direction finding) station to learn to operate the cathode ray set and take bearings on ships. This was a four week course, and after successfully passing out we were sent to HMS Flowerdown at Winchester to work on the DF station there. I well remember being on the middle watch the night of 6th June 1944 and seeing and hearing the squadrons and squadrons of aircraft droning overhead, thus realising that "something was up".

After taking and passing the PO's course at Scarborough we were drafted to Bower in Caithness to the DF station there. Travelling up on the "Jellicoe", the train left Euston for the Orkneys at 11.00 am. We reached Perth at 9.00 pm where we changed trains: all the service women were then carefully herded in to a separate carriage for the night. After an overnight journey we arrived in Thurso at

7.00 am the next morning.

The last six months of 1945 were spent at Bower and there we remained until we returned to Civvy Street in early 1946.

Never having spoken about our work – except perhaps when meeting up with an old shipmate – it never really became clear what we had been "up to" until a visit for the Bletchley Park Reunion in 1997. It was when, walking into a mock-up of a "Y" station receiving room, that nostalgia hit me like a ton of bricks. Then I realised I had been a very small cog in the wheel.

ROSEMARY LYSTER

In April 1940 at Scarborough Civilian Shore Wireless Station, as it was then called, I would sit tethered by earphones to my HRO in the Lower Receiving Room and hear "Control" at his desk directing his choice of D/F (Direction Finding) stations from the network sited from Lands End to Wick and Shetlands to take bearings of enemy ship or U-Boat transmissions. This was an urgent business as transmissions were very brief when German vessels had to break radio silence.

My own introduction to D/F came in November 1940 when four of us were drafted to work in a radio van parked on the top of Portsdown Hill above Cosham. There was just room for a W/T and a Special Duties (linguist) operator and the super Mister Millam, charge hand, during his visits. There were two radio sets and a very primitive hand-operated directional aerial which I was shown how to use on the job while listening for Channel traffic such as E-Boats.

This was going to be interesting and exciting. But after one week the four of us were recalled to Scarborough with (expletives deleted) a grim determination to get back to Portsdown Hill if at all possible.

Eventually, I achieved this in March 1941. If war was to interrupt training for my chosen profession then I wanted to be where the action was and there was plenty of that in Portsmouth, both enemy action and a much improved social life. Probably this was the happiest time of my six years in the Wrens.

A routine job for the W/Ts on the forenoon watch was to take bearings of the beams being set up to guide enemy bombers to that night's chosen target. At that time we had to take on watch with us the bare essentials we would need should the invasion materialise, in which case we were to join the Army in nearby Fort Widley. My diary records plenty of air raids and excitements, including a near-miss bomb outside our Quarters in Cosham but of course no reference to our work.

In July 1941 a call from Mr Moore ordered me to report in two days time for a special course at Flowerdown. With Chief Wrens Hanson, Jarred and Joy Collings the four of us had a concentrated introduction to the ways of radio propagation, the influence of the ionosphere, coast refraction, etc., the Adcock aerial system and finally Plessey and Marconi cathode ray D/F. My diary records that "Mr Hatch puts across the stuff in a very understandable way and it is interesting too".

After nine days, we were dispatched to Chicksands to live in The Priory's No 2 Lodge with Wren Cook Couldrey but no electricity or hot water. In Couldrey's absence we each cooked for ourselves when hungry, in my case mainly apple charlotte with fruit from the orchard.

While the new D/F station on Dead Man's Hill was being completed we worked watches in the small Naval Unit at the Priory. Collings and I biked up to see the D/F station, taking note of times and mileage – "possible but a bit tiring in wind and a hurry". First Officers Kemp and Garnier-Williams from HQ in London came to see about billets in Clophill, much nearer the D/F but found none so told us to look for our own which they would come to approve.

"Friday September 19. Tomorrow I start on the D/F 0800 – 1300. We have three days trial." Presumably we were considered competent. As the weeks passed the D/F hut, set between its four aerials in the middle of a huge ploughed field, acquired wood rails to enclose it, an armed sentry (following the visit of a Staff Officer Vulnerable Points), some paint to be followed by camouflage and gravel to improve the path from the road which I noted after a wet night as being fit only for ducks. The nearby "Rest" hut, containing an Elsan, became the Chargehand Mr Guy's home and workshop. So at night, when we were on in pairs from dusk to 0800 (a WRNS requirement, not popular) at the 0100 change of watch we would look for the glow of the sentry's cigarette and "disappear" on the other side of the hut! Our watches were 0800-1300, 1300-1830, 1830-0100 and 0100-0800. The forenoon watch was followed by one of the night watches, the next day another night watch, followed by a morning in bed and the 1300-1830. With luck we had the fourth day off. Not always, though. "Looking forward to tonight in bed. In thirteen nights I have only had four in a bed, the rest in the hut."

The only diary entry to refresh my memory of our duties is "There are 46 knobs on this instrument that I work and I know how to do them all!" The set with its cathode ray display screen, was built into the desk in front of us, a morse key and microphone direct line to Scarborough Control on the right. We "sat" on a prescribed frequency, which would change sometimes hourly, waiting for a ship to come up, usually a brief U-Boat report prefaced by E, known as E-bar. When one came we alerted Scarborough, giving frequency and type of signal, such as "E-bar", while at the same time taking a visual bearing of the signal, logging it and reporting our bearing to Scarborough when called. Our bearing, together with those taken by the other stations Control had ordered to that frequency, were telephoned to the Admiralty Duty Officer, hopefully providing a "cocked hat" indication of the position of the ship or U-Boat. When Chicksands was included in Scarborough's call to D/F on a frequency we were not waiting on we had to rush to the new frequency, pick up the almost completed transmission and get the best bearing possible. Seconds counted. The hut also had a bunk for the off-duty operator at night, a fireman's axe to cut the landline and sabotage the set and a loaded Webley revolver with extra rounds in a desk slot by our right hands, presumably to take out the fifth columnists or paratroopers who had eliminated or evaded the sentry. It provided endless entertainment for me on dull watches when, first unloaded, I used it to practice twirling cowboy skills. But it had its official purpose. "March 29 1942. Day of National Prayer. Had my three revolver rounds this morning. From 30 ft I hit his jugular and two somewhere round his lungs (a target, not Guy unfortunately)". Poor Mr Guy, out of favour at the time, probably dishing out extra watches owing to sickness or compassionate leave.

(Note. It was not usual practice for Wrens to be issued with guns and given the opportunity of target practice and later this was discontinued.)

Eventually we were billeted in Clophill, halving our cycle ride to the D/F. The only "invasion" that occurred was that of mice in

October 1943 following the harvest in our field which was assisted by three Italian POWs. After three day's noisy tunnelling the mice arrived in the hut. Their Lordships sanctioned the addition of a tortoiseshell kitten as residential watchkeeper. It slept on the operators' knees, climbing up via legs "regardless of silk stockings at 3 coupons and 7/6 per pair." In time a cat basket arrived from London, "a most wonderful contraption for a kitten which much prefers the desk, power pack or bunk."

In July 1943 I went to Penhallow C/R D/F (Cathode Ray Direction Finding) station, another hut in a field, near Perranporth and not far from my home in Marazion. Four of us were billeted in the most primitive of farmhouses, no electricity or running water. We washed in cold rainwater but were supplied with a jug of hot water when coming off night watch. Water for the loo, often out of action, depended on which farmer had switched the windmill two fields away to fill his house's header tank. The other operators there were Joan Yates, Jean Cameron and Renee Hill "and Dell living with the Blacksmith – at least billeted there".

We were fed mainly on farmhouse cake, bread, tinned meat and tinned salmon, no vegetables except Sundays. The Admiralty had installed a bath in the Rectory's cloakroom about ten minutes walk down the road, and provided the necessary coal from Falmouth Dockyard. It was not used much in the summer as we could cycle down the hill to swim at Perranporth. Here we wore blue shirts and bellbottoms unless warned by Mr Ingram the Chargehand that a Wren Officer from Falmouth planned to visit that day.

The D/F work was the same as at Chicksands. By January 1944 the fields and roads all round us were filling up with US troops and equipment assembling for the invasion. Their behaviour was excellent, we never felt worried by them in any way.

In June 1944 I left for OTC (Officers Training Course) at Stoke Poges, not Greenwich because of the flying bombs, and eventually, after a course at Eastleigh became a Fleet Air Arm Safety Equipment Officer.

Rosemary includes some extracts from her letters home which give some indication of some of the difficulties of the time.

April 9th 1941   Oakley House
                                              43 St. John's Road
                                                        Cosham

"Until last night nothing special has happened this week. There
was a slight raid on Monday night but the guns only woke me up
occasionally as I was so sleepy. Yesterday (Tuesday) I did nothing
out of the ordinary. Fitzmaurice went up to Winchester in the
Dispatch Rider's side car. She will not be back until tonight or
tomorrow probably. Hackney and Pat Russell and another girl went
up on watch and I retired to bed about 9.30 being asleep by about
10.30 though the guns kept me awake a bit to start with. Three
girls were sleeping at the back of the house, 3/0 Duncan in her
room and the cook and another girl in their rooms in the attic. I
was told afterwards that it was a very noisy night, but I only woke
up a few times with the guns rocking the house and a few bombs
I thought in the distance but it is difficult to tell which is which
really. Suddenly the house shook and I found myself under the
bedclothes with my arms over my face and head in the approved
style and glass showering all round on my bed while the house
shook. I waited quite happily for the rest of the house to fall but
nothing more happened. Glass kept tinkling about the place
outside, then silence. So I thought I had better get up in case I
had to dig out any bodies, slung my dressing gown on and tried
my bedroom slippers, but they were full of glass, so I just walked
barefoot across the room through piles of glass, quite unscathed,
while emptying my slippers on the way. I did not realise that I had
no need to open the door then, but later found it blown of its
hinges. In the passage I learned that all was well with the personnel
so I went back to change into trousers, sweater and shoes, took a
torch and climbed out of the front door which was barring my way
in a drunken manner having been blown off its hinges.

Outside there were lots of Wardens and I asked if anyone wanted
any help. A little boy came running to say a house on the corner
had been hit. We went round with the Wardens, wearing our tin
hats as the guns were still going and, though I seldom see shrapnel
that has come to earth, one or two bits are enough! Then I found
myself following a man into a house as he said he thought there
ought to be somebody about and I expected to have to help drag
out bloody corpses. But with three bombs and five to eight houses
badly damaged and lots of others not so badly there were no

casualties. One boy on a bike was slightly hurt but what he was doing about at 2.30 am unless on duty I don't know. One woman had hysterics I believe.

After about an hour wandering about with police and wardens, examining the hole in the road etc., we went back to bed. The garage doors were gone so I padlocked my bike and removed my boots and coat (uniform) from the little lobby by the front door as that was gone too, and the window. My coat has great holes in it but I shall get a new coat or have them mended for me.

When we went back to bed I could not get to sleep to start with because, a) the bed was full of glass which is uncomfortable to turn on and the pillow was ingrained with it too, b) the cat had evidently checked its headlong flight and come home again because it was crying pitifully but too loudly, c) the Wardens would keep walking about outside and coming to the door to peer in – no difficulty – and, d) the ceiling in the room below kept falling at odd intervals. Then at seven the milkman came and said in a loud voice, "You won't be wanting any milk will you?" and the cook replied in an equally loud voice that we were still alive and of course wanted milk. So after a bit I got up and the rest of the house who had not gone on watch got up too and we began to work. The first thing I discovered was that the top had been blown off my powder and it was full of powdered and broken glass. I can deal with it though. Also the rubber and spines had jumped out of the wooden back and handle of Fritz's hairbrush! Impossible!

Eventually, Hackney came off watch and together we swept and dusted our room and remade all three beds, shaking the sheets and blankets out of the windows. This was not difficult as I had removed all the remaining glass. We had to take up the linoleum, move and dust everything and even then it was still dirty. A steward came and washed it afterwards but they are mending the ceiling this afternoon so it won't be so good. We found a bit of bomb in our chest of drawers and something must have zoomed past my bed because it broke the mirror on the door of the built-in cupboard. Also there were holes in the ceiling but I think the bits went right up. The ceiling over the chest of drawers all fell down, the upstairs lavatory is cracked, leaking and unusable but otherwise the three back rooms are O.K. The kitchen was a mess. But the eggs were not broken which was a great thing!

All sorts of officials came, about the telephone, Oakley to be blacked out before anything else was done, so gangs of men came up from the Dockyard putting transparent material in the windows. I went outside to help Mr Millam remove all the hedge which had been cut and blasted down and tidy up the place generally. I found the fuse and nosecap of the bomb. The hole in the road was quite small. The Warden said the road being so hard the blast had all gone outwards. I never heard the three bombs coming and when it did fall and the house started collapsing I can quite truthfully say that I was not in the least frightened. I was surprised that they should have dropped anything while I was around as I usually scare them, and then I was surprised that the house did not collapse altogether. My bed was warm, I had plenty of blankets on top and felt perfectly safe!

There is some talk of us giving a bottle party on Friday week. Of course it is my 'Waterloo' but I shall be able to be there for a bit..."

Rosemary enjoyed the excitement of the Portsdown Hill Station, in comparison, life at Chicksands was rather dull. There were few amusements apart from cycling to Bedford cinema, the odd game of tennis and occasional Service dance, and some riding at a yard north of Bedford. "There was nothing glamorous or exciting about the life compared with Portsdown Hill".."Once the invasion scare was over, the work at Chicksands was transferred to Ventor in the Isle of Wight – it played an important part in the run up to and during D-Day under the supervision of 3/0 "Fish" Crawshaw who joined up with me in January 1940."

"In Chicksands in November 1942 we were told by Lt. Wright that "we had a very good reputation here as a crew." By this time Rosemary was the senior operator so had to 'supervise' in addition to normal watches, deal with Wren H.Q., billets for new arrivals (if the leavers billets took the opportunity to opt out!) ration books etc. She says, "Billet finding was a real chore", and adds, "No one of course, told us if our work was valuable – we did not "need to know"!

CHAPTER 8

WRENS OVERSEAS

This is part of the story of the first draft of Wrens to go overseas in the Second World War.

JOAN DINWOODIE (nee SPRINKS)

On January 8th 1940 the first class of 24 Wrens to train as Wireless Telegraphists reported to the Training and Drafting Depot, King's College, Campden Hill Road, Kensington. The course was expected to take six months and the weekly payment would be 33/6d of which £1 per week would be deducted for board and lodging. The first class was of mixed experience – some had none and some were already trained telegraphists, whilst two had served in the same category in World War One. They came from widely differing backgrounds and locations. The two Royal Naval instructors were C.P.O. Gillie and P.O. Redman. The Officer-in-Charge of the Depot was First Officer Buckmaster and the P.T. Officer Third Officer Vida Wallace-Smith (now Lady Christison). Life at the Depot consisted of morse, drill, P/T., assorted lectures, darkening ship etc. One morning the Wrens had time off to go and cheer the crews of "AJAX", "ACHILLES" and "EXETER" at their triumphal parade after the battle of the River Plate. Most importantly we signed the Official Secrets Act.

The following classes were smaller and slightly revised. The second and subsequent classes (by then at the Royal Naval College, Greenwich) under pressure did the six months course in three. When trained we could choose to be sent to W/T Stations in the north (Scarborough) or South (HMS FLOWERDOWN, Winchester). We were given brass buttons and rated Chief Wrens so to be equal in status to the civilian men's trade union. At Scarborough we were billeted in boarding houses and walked or cycled to go on watch in a room that was below ground. The night watch took a lot of getting used to – from 11.30pm until 8am, sitting at a bench with a number of ex-naval personnel who all seemed to consume very strong tea and to smoke endless 'ticklers' (rolled tobacco). There was no fresh air at all, and in addition there was of course a total blackout. Everything was so secret that we were trusted not to breathe a word about the work we were doing. From these main stations, Wrens were sent off to man smaller stations, also engaged in very secret work. The Wrens at Flowerdown were billeted in Littleton village and one of them remembers that on every Middle Watch the Home Guard Sergeant escorted her to work via the local for half a pint for him – none for the Wren of course. During the Southampton blitz they could see the fires burning and the village had a direct hit, with lives lost nearby. The five Wrens on duty all went on working stoically during the raid and ALL the men had dived under the tables!

In the Autumn of 1940 a call went out to the various W/T 'Y' Stations in the UK for WRNS volunteers to serve overseas. We learned later that this was to be in Singapore – at the W/T Station at Kranji. Selection boards were held at Queen Anne's Mansions in London, with Dame Vera Laughton-Matthews, Mrs Bell and Lady Cholmondeley interviewing the applicants. This was at the height of the London Blitz. From the large number of volunteers, the following twenty were chosen:-

Joyce Allingham	Tolleshunt D'Arcy, Essex
May Blood	Newbury, Berks.
Henrietta Marshall	Edgware, Middx.
Joan Sprinks	Norwich, Norfolk
Margaret Finch	Scarborough, Yorks.
Margaret Hodgson	Bickley, Kent
Rene Skipp	Northwood, Middx.
Monica Armstrong	Walton-on-Thames, Surrey
Lillie Gadd	Epsom, Surrey
Jean Epps	Kingsbury, Middx.
Marjorie Finlay	Liverpool, Lancs
Joan Barber	Bournmouth, Dorset
Enid Monson	Acton, London
Eileen Moorley	Derby
Elizabeth Miller	Newbury, Berks
Betty Dart	Starcross, Devon
Phyllis Holmes	Ross-on-Wye, Hereford
Doris Jackson	Doncaster, Yorks
Catherine Burrows	Epsom, Surrey
Connie Heap	Derby

In January 1941, we reported to the Royal Naval College, Greenwich for a special course under civilian instructors. Most of this instruction was interrupted constantly by having to go down to the air raid shelters and after a while we spent every night in hammocks or on mattresses in the cellars under the College. During this time we got to know each other better and met the officer who was to be in charge of us – Second Officer Betty Archdale, who had been a barrister and captain of the Women's Cricket Team to tour Australia in the nineteen thirties.

(Note: Helen Elizabeth (Betty) Archdale MBE died 11 Jan 2000 at Killawara NSW Australia. First Officer WRNS 1940-46. Served Yarmouth, Singapore, Colombo, Ceylon, Kenya, Persian Gulf, Australia. In charge of the first draft of Wrens to serve overseas and awarded MBE for getting them safely out of Singapore before the Japanese invaded).

In early February we were given our tropical uniforms and taken to the Admiralty to have tea and meet Princess Marina of Kent, the First Sea Lord, Admiral Sir Charles Little and the First Lord of the Admiralty, Mr A.V. Alexander. These uniforms were made from a very heavy white drill material, white cotton stockings, and wide-brimmed navy blue hat with cover, white canvas shoes and a topee, the latter being an object of great mirth when we finally arrived in Singapore. One (ribald) remark at the tea party suggested that we only needed two pennies in our eyes and we'd be ready to be laid out – so AWFUL were the uniforms.

Vaccinations, inoculations, lectures on what we could expect from our service in the tropics completed our preparations and we returned to Scarborough to await our ship. On the 3rd March 1941 we left by train for Glasgow, changing trains at York. An elderly porter there (lugging our unlabelled baggage) asked where we were going and we all shouted that it was a secret. His reply was unprintable – he only wanted to know which platform we were going from! Arriving in Glasgow we were greeted by the Lord Provost and entertained by him to the pantomime "Ali Baba" at the Empire Theatre. We spent the night at the YWCA. The next day, March 4th, we sailed from Greenock, where the convoy had assembled, in the Blue Funnel ship "Nestor". There were about fifty other ships, mostly cargo boats and tankers and the aircraft carrier "Argus", cruisers and corvettes. On March 8th a lone Focke Wolfe "Condor" aircraft attacked the convoy, dropping several bombs fairly near but not apparently scoring a hit. They were near enough for two of us to finish a whole box of "Black Magic" chocolates, very precious in those days, just in case we and they went to the bottom. The next day we left the convoy and headed south on our own. During the journey and even in the roughest weather, the twenty Wrens turned up for every single meal. Sometimes we were the only ones in the dining saloon, causing our disgruntled steward to moan that it would be just his luck to have twenty good sailors while the other stewards were all playing cards because their passengers were sick!

We believe that the rest of the convoy was later severely mauled by U-boats and suffered many losses, so we were very lucky. It was also the time that the "Scharnhorst" and "Gneisenau" (German battleships) were prowling the parts of the ocean through which we passed. During this time we had morse practice everyday, Malay lessons and took turns at the lookout stations. Four of us celebrated 21st birthdays on this part of the voyage.

After four weeks we sailed into Cape Town in the early morning – a lovely sight. We had a day ashore, stocking up with fruit and chocolate, neither of which we had seen for ages. The next day we sailed up the south east coast to Durban, where it took three days to coal ship and we were able to go shopping, swimming and visit the famous 'Valley of 1000 Hills' in Zululand. We then had a wonderful trip across the Indian Ocean. It was considered a less dangerous area and we even had small blue lights on deck, though we altered course once at the sight of a starshell. Our next port of call was Penang, where we marched behind the sailors to the Pay Office, receiving a payment of five dollars (about 11/8d). We then had a trip around the island and our first swim in the lukewarm tropical water. The "Nestor" then sailed down the Malacca Strait, visiting Port Swettenham and Kuala Lumpur and eventually reached Singapore on April 20th.

The Royal Naval W/T Station, Kranji, was quite separate from the Naval Base and a long way from the harbour and city – quite near the Jahore Causeway to the north. Our mess and quarters had been built specially for Civilian Shore Wireless Service personnel but reallocated to us. The buildings were on 6ft. concrete pillars and six of us were accommodated in each block, each with a well-furnished room, bathroom and small verandah. A Chinese 'Amah' was provided for each block for cleaning amd dhobying. The space under the block was a happy hunting ground for frogs and was presumably to discourage snakes etc. and to cope with the sudden tropical downpours. The Mess had a large room for meals, a small games room, a large verandah and a kitchen beneath it. There was a large bamboo hedge all round. As soon as possible we had new, lighter uniforms made, together with a working rig of white drill skirt and a cool cotton blouse.

Kranji W/T Station was a very happy 'ship'. Besides the Wrens there were sailors of the Malayan Navy, soldiers, civilian, Army and RAF personnel and we all mixed very happily together, except in the station swimming pool where no mixed bathing was permitted. We were divided into four watches, working roughly naval watches, shorter than those we had been used to in the UK. I think all of us would agree that being in the watchroom at Kranji was the hottest time any of us is likely to experience. The heat had to be experienced to be believed. We were in a concrete building with no windows, no air-conditioning (we were told it had been sunk on the way out to the station), constantly manned 24 hours a day so that it was never aired, additional heat from the sets and a haze and smell of smoking that could almost be cut with a knife. No wonder that we went on watch armed with giant flaskes of iced 'ayer lima' (lime water) and small towels to wrap around our necks to absorb as much as possible of the constant sweat. The tropical heat of Singapore seemed almost cool by comparison when we emerged from watchkeeping.

In July we were joined by ten more Chief Wrens who had been destined for Alexandria but were diverted at Durban to join us. They were;

May Atkinson, Freda Bonner, Mollie Crace, Beryl Crace, Pamela Gray, Betty Kopsen, Joan Peters, Kathleen Moore, Jean Porter, Penelope Rogers.

In August we were deeply saddened to hear of the loss of the third overseas draft to Gibraltar. Twelve of them were fellow telegraphists and seven others cypher officers, together with a Naval nursing sister, and had sailed in the SS 'Aguila' of the Yeoward Line and had been torpedoed by U-201 (Lt.Schnee) in waters to the west of the Bay of Biscay, the ship sinking in less than a minute with very few survivors. Some of these girls had been on watch with us at Scarborough. We could hardly believe it. They were all really nice girls and first class operators. In spite of their fate, further volunteers were immediately called for, obtained very quickly and sent to Gibraltar as replacements as soon as possible. After the war, relatives, friends and members of the WRNS raised enough money to buy a lifeboat named the 'Aguila Wren' in memory of these girls. It was launched on June 28th 1952 at Aberystwyth.

On December 7th 1941 the Japanese attacked Pearl Harbour and during the night there were raids on Singapore. We were so busy during this time that one of our number on watch was amazed to see and hear that war had been declared until, coming off watch, we could see and hear the Japanese planes in the clear night sky. Some of the others were at the Cathay cinema when a notice flashed on the screen ordering all Service personnel to report immediately to their units. We didn't get out again until we were evacuated a month later, except for one Wren shopping for us all. It was impossible to enforce a complete blackout, but even the 'brownout' made us swelter even more. On the 10th December we were shattered to hear of the sinking of the 'Prince of Wales' and 'Repulse' off the east coast of Malaya and on the 15th the surviving Royal Marines from the ships were sent to Kranji and being naturally trigger happy after such an experience caused us more anxiety sometimes than the air raids.

With the deteriorating military situation it was decided to evacuate the Commander-in-Chief's staff further westward to Ceylon, partly we believe because of our specialist experience which would have been difficult to replace at short notice. We left Kranji on January 5th 1942 on board the troopship 'Devonshire', accompanied by HMT 'Lancashire', two destroyers and two cruisers. The food was pretty grim, the bread and porridge being full of weevils, but who were we to complain about such a minor detail. As the Japanese had by this time driven a long way down the Malayan peninsula we were unable to take the usual route through the Straits of Malacca and headed south through the Banka and Sunda Straits and thence to Colombo, arriving on January 15th.

We were quartered in Galle road, Colpetty, near Colombo, very near the sea. The kitchens were most un-hygienic with piles of raw meat covered with flies lying on the floor. Working conditions were quite good. One of us would leave half an hour before the change of watch to 'shake' the relieving operators and this involved walking past long lines of rickshaw men, sleeping near their vehicles with only their coconut oil lamps to light our way.

On Easter Sunday, April 5th, a large force of Japanese bombers attacked Colombo. Fortunately the harbour had been cleared as this had been expected, although several ships, including the cruisers 'Dorsetshire' and 'Cornwall', had been sunk southwest of Ceylon. Our house servants promptly stole our bikes and headed upcountry. We had a good look at one of the crashed Jap dive bombers which had been shot down near us. In view of these events, part of Admiral Somerville's Force A was sent to the Seychelles for refuelling and thence on to Mombasa. It was one of the biggest thrills of our service to be part of this fleet. We embarked in the AMC 'Alaunia', surrounded by many ships of the Eastern Fleet – HMS 'Warspite' the flagship, the carriers 'Indomitable' and 'Formidable', the cruisers 'Emerald', 'Newcastle' and many others and as the voyage proceeded took part in many naval manoevres. On deck one day when the rum ration was being issued, we asked, "What about us, don't we get any?". "No, love", the Master-at-Arms said, "You are on the ship's books as Boys and while you're in the tropics you'll get your share of lime juice, same as the young lads".

We arrived in Kilindini Harbour, Mombasa, on the 3rd May 1942 to an accompanying welcome of wolf-whistles from HMS 'Royal Sovereign' and were quartered in a small hotel in Mombasa – the 'Lotus'. We worked in what had been an Indian Boys' School and overlooked an African military prison camp, which view was compensated for by a wonderful view of the Indian Ocean. Our watchroom was constantly plagued by masses of flying insects (including praying mantises) and bats. We cursed the Arab dhows that came in from the sea beating drums so loud that we couldn't read signals at times.

At this time we were issued with hideous thigh-length canvas leggings and cotton sleeves to be worn after 6pm. as an anti-malarian protection. Needless to say they didn't stay on long after leaving our quarters. By now, more and more Wrens were arriving from UK (all different categories) and we originals were drafted home in three parties.

The first draft was torpedoed when the 'Empress of Canada' was sunk on 14th March 1943 in the Southern Atlantic by the Italian submarine 'Leonardo Da Vinci' (Lt.Cdr. Gazzana). The six were Bonner, Finch, Crace M., Gadd, Gray and Kopsen. All were eventually saved although some were afloat for up to four days on rafts and lifeboats. Before the attack they had been seeing upturned lifeboats and wreakage from torpedoed ships and then it was their turn. After torpedoes hit the engine-room, it filled rapidly with water and after a list to starboard the order "Abandon Ship" was given. Many burned their hands through sliding down ropes into life-rafts. The U-Boat surfaced and took off an Italian doctor. The Wrens could see sharks and barracudas knifing among the people in the water and several were bitten but when a Sunderland flying boat was sighted they knew that help would be on the way and toward the fourth evening at sunset HMS 'Boreas' came and picked up survivors. They were landed at Freetown but nearly 400 were lost. The official report by Captain Goold said that the conduct of Chief Wren Bonner in a lifeboat was worthy of the highest praise as were the other three Wrens in the same boat. They greatly assisted the officers of the 'Empress of Canada' while awaiting rescue. Chief Wren Gadd found herself alone on a life-raft with 12 sailors before being rescued. Freda Bonner was so impressed by the courage and gallantry that she had seen that she determined to become a doctor after the war and indeed studied at the Harvard School of Public Health in Boston, becoming a head of Public Health in the West Indies and in charge of a hospital in Sydney later. This draft eventually reached home in the 'Mauretania'.

(Note: The 'Leonardo Da Vinci' was sunk on 23rd May 1943 northeast of the Azores by HM Ships 'Active' and 'Ness'.)

The next draft of seven – Barber, Burrows, Epps, Finlay, Holmes, Skipp and Sprinks, sailed from Mombasa in the 'Arundel Castle', in a small convoy with the 'City of Paris', 'Maloja' and a Dutch ship, accompanied by the cruiser 'Devonshire'. During the voyage to Durban there were several cases of typhus, resulting in some deaths. We were detailed to go round the cabins killing off the lice and bugs! On arrival we were taken in buses to the hospital and scrubbed all over with lysol, all our clothes and possessions being heaped in one large pile. When nearing home in the Bay of Biscay the ship was attacked by a Focke Wolfe aircraft and we had to gather on the first deck with emergency kit. One senior Officer's wife asked us to help her with her fur coat and extra cases, but we made it plain that we would be helping mothers with small children. Fortunately, fog descended and with the fire from the Gerliken guns, the pilot decided not to pursue the action. The third draft had an uneventful voyage home except for our first case of malaria probably caught ashore in Dar-es-Salaam.

After leave, we all met again at a WRNS establishment in Golden Square near Piccadilly, then after a refresher course at New College, Finchley Road, Hampstead, allocated different categories (needs had changed). Some were selected as instructors, some given commissions in other branches, some sent overseas again in the same or different work to South Africa, Ceylon, India, Kenya, Basra and Australia. One, (Beryl Crace) was later lost in the Indian Ocean with her husband and baby son when the 'Khedive Ismail' was sunk by a Japanese Submarine. After getting a commission, Phyllis Holmes in 1945 had the awful job (for the Director of Naval Intelligence) of collecting evidence in ten Bombay and Bangalore Hospitals about the attrocities committed by the Japanese against their prisoners of war. She found several people we had known in Singapore and she and her fellow Wren officers had to listen to horrifying stories from former prisoners. This made her realise how lucky we were to have been evacuated as the Japanese would never have shown us any mercy, especially considering the work we had been doing.

Now in 1988, some of us have died and we are spread over many parts of the world. The oldest (a First World War Wren) was 90 in 1987. Some have lost their husbands and some have celebrated their Ruby Weddings. During our service we were lucky in many ways. We saw so many beautiful parts of the world that we wouldn't normally have visited. When we had leave we were given hospitality on rubber estates, tea plantations, game reserves in Kenya, etc. We were very healthy and had very little illness; we escaped injury though we had many brushes with enemy action, we made friendships that have lasted with great affection to the present day (twelve of us still meet at intervals) and we wouldn't have missed it for worlds.

Our experiences have given us a great admiration for and loyalty to the Royal Navy and for all our lives we will feel a great affinity with that rightly named Senior Service. It was a great privilege to be part of it for the wartime years.

125

WE KEPT THE SECRET

(Note: Many service women and nurses lost their lives while on active service, but you do not find their names on any town or village war memorials. I wonder why? G.P.)

ANN McNISH (continued from Chapter 1)

Then Ceylon. As I had conections there I applied for a draft. I was sent to the Clyde to join the 'Alcantara'. On to Bombay, there transferred to the 'Polaski', a Polish ship and a seven days wait in a monsoon. We were not allowed ashore. It was miserable. At last on to Ceylon, our convoy was attacked and a merchantman went down. We eventually arrived in Colombo and discovered the smell of the East. We were now in white uniform issued at Crosby Hall. The accommodation was better than expected. We worked at HMS 'Anderson' with sailors, but the work was hard. I hadn't been in Colombo many days when HMS Renown arrived, the flagship of Admiral Sir John Power. A message arrived at Kent House where I was quartered, from my brother-in-law with an invitation to a tea dance on board. This was followed by lunch on another day in the Ward Room. Dusty Duristerville, my brother-in-law was Signals Officer and was by this time ashore. I often saw him at 'Anderson'.

Colombo was the greatest fun swimming at Mount Lavinia, the fleet coming in and out. Dancing at the 'Silver Fawn' night club, the GOH (Grand Orient Hotel) and the Galle Face Hotel. Curry at Pilawi, (in the Pettah, or native bazaar). Then Peace. The Kent House Wrens led the whole V.J. parade past Lord Mountbatton which was an honour. The repatriation ships carrying the ex-prisoners of war from the Japanese camps started to arrive in Colombo. We were detailed off to help at the Echlon barracks where they were received. The civilians were a sorry sight. I ran into a man I had known as a child in Hong Kong. He stayed overnight in Colombo and I dined with him. Next it was my turn to pack for home, not knowing when exactly I would be leaving. I went in the 'Athlone Castle'. On arriving at Southampton, we all queued at the telephone to ring home. Then it was on to Stockgrove Park for luggage and discharge papers, etc. and the end of four and a half years of memorable service as a Wren. I did get a 'hook' and two stripes.

Whilst in Ceylon I went up to my family's tea estate and saw the tea factory at Choisy.

Ann says she has a wonderful scrap book of souvenirs including

Mount Lavinia beach, a favourite leisure spot

her 'call up' papers and discharge and lots of pictures and other souvenirs, a reminder of some happy times.

SYLVIA PULLEY (nee BATES) (continued from Chapter 2)

I had volunteered for service in Ceylon and was posted there in 1945, travelling out on the 'Esperance Bay'. Gwendoline Page was also on that ship. She could sing and was in great demand at the ship's concert.

I lived in Belvoir House (Colombo) and bused into HMS Anderson where we did four hourly watches. I had just started to learn about the Japanese Code, when a little more than a week later it was all over. I had by this time been promoted to Petty Officer, and was moved from Belvoir to Kent House, which unfortunately meant I was separated from most of my friends. Off duty life was very good. Socially the Wrens were in great demand which meant we were able to see a great deal of that beautiful country. Being a Petty Officer I had to do an evening duty once a month in Regulating Office. This meant checking in the Wrens with late passes. When you went out in the evening you had to sign in the book, who was your escort and where you were going. An interesting occupation while you were waiting for the late passes to return, was to see how many times a certain male had escorted different Wrens, and particularly one who might have escorted you!

We were young and to most of us it was a great adventure, but it was here that the real tragedy of war hit me. Wrens not on duty were helping the Red Cross with the returning prisoners of war from the Japanese camps. Those well enough to come ashore were given new clothing and entertained by many Wrens. I was sorting mail in the ballroom of Government House. The ships were in the harbour for little more than twenty four hours. As they arrived we would receive a list of those on board, not in alphabetical order, and we sorted through the thousands of telegrams and letters, working well into the night if necessary. Two of us took the mail out to the ship on a Naval launch. Here we were surrounded by the men who were not well enough to go ashore. They were eager to talk, and wanted to know what things were like back home. Those who were so very sick, lay in rows on the deck too ill to care. Today this remains so vividly in my mind.

The Clock Tower, Colombo. A well known meeting place.

GWENDOLINE PAGE (nee ACASON)
(Continued from Chapter 2)

At the end of my embarkation leave I was told to report to New College and there met up with about 50 others also destined for overseas. I recognised one other girl from B.P. and together Eileen and I went through the medical check ups, innoculations, etc. The result of many varied innoculations at one go were noticeable next morning on parade, when a number of them fell out, flat on their faces! Those of us who were not carted off to sick bay, were given the task of emptying the fire buckets and refilling them with fresh water. With sore and aching arms we went about this (considered by us) cruel task, but no doubt there was a reliable reason for such madness, though at the time we rather wished we had joined those in sick bay!

The day came when we were told of our destination. It was to be the fabulous, tropical island of Ceylon. The tear drop at the foot of India, or original Garden of Eden as it was called. Time was given for the news to sink in and excitement to subside before practical details were outlined. From then on we were confined to quarters, mail was censored of course and no phone calls.

Tropical uniforms were issued along with talks on health, etc. Then came the day when along with kitbags, trunks and still carrying gas masks, we once more clambered into trucks to take us to a port and our first view of sea, ships and sailors. The first stage was Waterloo Station where along with other troops overloaded with kit, we were put on to a train bound for Southampton. The Wrens being in a carriage carefully segregated from the Marines and other troops.

At the docks we were lined up and stood at ease in an area which provided an overall view of the 'Esperance Bay' the ship on which we were to travel, and watched the others going aboard. At last it was our turn and brought to attention, we were then directed to an upper gang-plank and carrying our belongings negotiated its narrow way on board ship. There were 5 girls sharing a cabin intended for two where I was berthed, but we were well off compared to the men who were quartered in the hold.

I cannot say the voyage was comfortable, in fact in the dreadful heat of the Red Sea with no breeze what-so-ever it was decidedly uncomfortable. Sadly one of the stokers died of heat exhaustion and we experienced a funeral at sea.

Finally after several weeks we awoke one morning to find our ship anchored in Colombo Harbour and new scents of vegetation wafted to us across the water. The busy harbour was alive with ships and small boats, some of which were already ferrying troops ashore, while cranes deposited luggage in barges alongside. Soon came our turn to make our way down metal steps on the ship's side into other barges. These took us ashore to waiting trucks ready to carry us on the next stage of the journey. It took a little time to adjust our legs to walking on land again, but all were eager to see more of this tropical island.

Our quarters were in the grounds of a large, colonial house in low, palm thatched, cement buildings called 'Bandas'. A Banda was divided into two rooms with seven girls in each section. (A separate room was built on the end of each Banda for a Petty Officer). Each girl had an iron bed, small bedside locker and a mosquito net. The mosquito net was useful in not only keeping off the mosquitoes, but in protecting one from the variety of insects which fell from the thatch. We also learnt that it was wise to check for other things such as scorpions which sometimes scuttled across the floor or nestled in shoes. The ablutions were in other blocks of buildings as was the dining mess. This was surrounded by wire netting to stop the big, black, arrogant crows stealing food from the plates.

After one day to settle in, Wrens were dispersed to various jobs. I was one who was to work at 'HMS Anderson', an interception and decoding station just outside Colombo. The Wren Officer introduced me to the Sub.Lieut. in charge of the watch saying, "Sub.Lieut Page will be your Duty Officer from now on". Little did she know she had started, for he is still my duty officer!

The watch consisted of five Wrens and five Ratings with a Leading Hand nicknamed "Tubby" for obvious reasons. My job differed from Bletchley Park as this office was a signals distributing office and my job was to sort the signals to pass to the offices concerned. A civilian Cable and Wireless man, Mr Bennet seemed to be the overall head of the section.

The first thing that struck me was the more relaxed atmosphere which prevailed in contrast to that of Bletchley Park, although all seemed to be getting on with the work. When I had been introduced to the Sub.Lieut. I had given a smart salute and replied, "Yes Sir" or, "No Sir" to his questions, but after the Wren Officer had left, he surprised me by saying, "Drop the 'Sir'. My name is Harry".

Street scene in Colombo

The times of the watch also differed from B.P. We worked a system of 24 hour watch instead of the week of nights, week of evenings and week of days. This meant being woken at unearthly times like 2.30am in order to be on watch again at 4am. The only advantage being the 24 hours rest day before the next duty began.

When we were due for a long leave, there was the opportunity to travel to the service leave camps in the hills. Situated near the village of Diyatalawa, between 3000 to 6000ft above sea level, where the climate was refreshingly cool after the humidity of the coast and the scenery was not only grand but beautiful. It was a wonderful place to relax and renew ones faded energy. I had become engaged to marry Harry by this time, and we managed to fit our leave times together, he booked to stay at the Officer's leave centre while I stayed at the Wrens centre. We hitched a ride up in the back of a truck sitting on packing cases, not exactly comfortable but quite exciting with some marvellous views of the countryside as we climbed higher and higher into the hills. The accommodation was in small chalet type rooms with beautiful views from the small verandah outside the door. Each morning I woke to a perfect day, but being the beginning of the monsoon season we found that it was wise to be under cover by two o'clock each day when the rain arrived. The rain swamped everything and soon turned paths into running rivers of water, but some time during the night it stopped and by the time we arose the next morning, everything was dry and we were presented with another perfect morning!

A rather ramshackle cinema was available to us in which the bats flew around beneath its roof. We soon learnt to take our rain coats with us, not to protect us from the rain, but to protect us from the bugs in the cane seats which bit our bare legs and arms if we had nothing between them and the cane! Without the coats we came away with lines of little red bites on the back of thighs and along our arms. There were intervals when the film stopped abruptly in mid scene, the lights went up and Sinhalese attendants came around to patrons carrying trays of tea. Once the interval was over the lights went off and the film began again where it had left off.

There was also a club house where one could have coffee or a drink from the bar. A piano resided in this room and impromptu dances could be held with the help of anyone capable of playing it. Boogie and Jive being popular at this time.

Harry and I fell in love with this area and returned in 1957 with our two children to enjoy again its wonderful climate, bustling market, friendly people and lovely countryside.

Our journey back to HMS Anderson after our leave was rather more exciting than I had bargained for. The rains had become more persistant and the roads were more slippery. This did not seem to worry our native driver, who took the steep winding roads at a fast pace, until on rounding one s-bend the truck skidded and slewed across the road with the back ending up about six inches from the edge of a precipice. The driver turned around and laughed when he saw that all his passengers were still with him, but I had a headache the rest of the way down and did not relax until we had passed through the curtain of humid air which signalled that we were back on the coastal plain once more!

During the first month or two of my time in Ceylon, the Atom bombs were dropped on Japan. This resulted in the end of hostilities and the finish of enemy signals. On August 15th, V.J. Day was celebrated by a March Past on the sea front of Colombo with Lord Louis Mountbatten taking the salute.

After this there was little work for us to do and when the Prisoners of War in Malaya and Japan had been released, we Wrens were asked to help receive them in our off duty time as the ships carrying the ex-P.O.W.s put into Colombo harbour for provisions on their way home. Many were in a very poor state physically and also were worried about their reception at home, for they had had little contact with their families and had had years of being brainwashed by their Japanese captors. They did not recognise our uniforms and the thought of women officers astounded them beyond belief! I believe we were able to put some of their fears at rest and gave them some idea of the changes that had taken place while they had been away. Most of all I hope we were able to reassure them of the warm welcome awaiting them at home. Once all the Prisoners of War had left, it became the turn of the service women in Ceylon to return to UK, but I for one was sad to leave the sunshine of this beautiful island.

Note: A fuller account of my time in the WRNS is given in my book GROWING PAINS – A Teenager's War.

MARGARET SHARMAN (nee JOHNSON) died 3rd April 2002

I wish I could say it was I who exclaimed, 'All I ask is a tall ship' to the WRNS recruiting officer, but alas, that inspiration belongs to a cartoonist of the period: the tall willowly maiden of his drawing, confronting the baffled-looking Wren officer, was as unlike my cowed self as it was possible to be. It was the recruiting officer who decided that I should be a Radio Mechanic, 'mobile', and ready for action. She almost demanded that I leave the office 'at the double'.

In no time I was 'instructed to report for training as a Probationary Wren', joining the 900 Wrens and pro-Wrens at Mill Hill. It all seemed to be a continuation of boarding school: there was reveille and lights out, and square-bashing took the place of games. We had our hair cut and examined for nits; we wore an ill-fitting 'orphan annie', officially described as 'one blue overall .... in the form of a coat dress (which) constitutes sufficient wear for indoors of a uniform nature'. The doctor noted the state of our skin, eyes, ears, and asked embarrassing questions about diseases. We sat in classrooms for instruction in saluting, recognition of other services' ranks, and what a galley, foc'sle and quarterdeck were. There were parts of the grounds where you had to run, and other places where you must always walk. You had to salute the flag. Mill Hill, I discovered later, prepared you for life in a port, not for my first destination in the civilian heart of Essex. I didn't encounter this orthodoxy again until I was demobbed at Chatham nearly three years later.

The actual building, Ridgeway, Mill Hill, was immense – seven stories high, and my cabin was right at the top – a long way to trudge when you had forgotten your book, or your cigarettes (we became smokers as a matter of course). The war went on undisturbed by our presence, and I nonchalently told my parents in rural Shropshire, "the gunfire is rather fine".

At my first interview I discovered that I couldn't be a Radio Mech because it was a 'closed category'. So perhaps I would like to become a Classifier, which would suit me because of my school maths record. What did a Classifier do? The Wren officer couldn't tell me until I had signed the Official Secrets Act. And how could I accept or refuse to be one if I didn't know what the job entailed? It was all very mystifying. Eight Wrens were to be chosen for this honour, and the twelve or so of us being interviewed were forbidden to discuss it, even amongst ourselves. We didn't have much time to anyway, what with daily squad drill, cleaning the 'ship', and cutting Lyons lemon-curd Swiss rolls into a dozen slim slices for 900 teas (I made myself sick eating the end bits).

A second interview, my signature on the Official Secrets Act, and I was an embryo Classifier, with a new designation, Wren Johnson M.B., 65872 and a uniform. It took me hours to dress for the passing-out parade, for which I felt I should be immaculate because I was 'squad marker'. History doesn't relate how many grubby stiff collars I discarded after trying to coax them into place with collar-studs and tie. What a relief when I discovered you could buy paper ones! The eight of us were finally packed off in a truck for Beehive Lane, Chelmsford where a Victorian house enveloped 60 Wrens, most of whom were living in three Nissen huts in the garden. It was now late Autumn, and at night we froze in the hut unless someone lit the cylindrical stove in the middle, when we sweated. Two girls had to get up for the fire-watching duty if the sirens sounded, while the rest of us got used to planes and ack-ack guns. The images that remain in my memory are of a Wren who found a nest of mice in a neat hole in her cardigan and threw them alive onto the stove: and of having become complacent about air-raids after ten days or so without any, and deciding to wash my hair while on fire-watching duty. Never do that. The sirens sounded, and I stumbled through the dark grounds until the all-clear for signs of fire-bombs, with cold, cold soapsuds dripping down my nose from under a tin hat.

We cycled or walked every morning for the first three weeks to the Marconi Works, for more lectures, this time specifically on the ionosphere, Heaviside layer and radio carrier waves. I spent my 16/- a week pay on visits to Chelmsford cinema and tea (with jam and cakes – luxury!) at the Women's Services Club, which we were able to visit more often once we had passed our exams and were put on watches, two of us on each. We took thick corned beef sandwiches to see us through night watch – it is strange how I remember the food so well!

I enjoyed Chelmsford but, wasn't there for more than two months before being drafted to Scarborough, and together with Iris Coltman, who had accompanied me all the way so far, was billeted with Mrs Thompson, who specialised in providing endless cups of tea and toast, and a warm fire in her sitting room. The main

Wrenery was at the Hotel Cecil on Ryndleside, where we ate large meals and waited for transport to take us on our watches to the W/T Station. The work here was totally different – no more ionosphere, no more diagrams of radio signals bouncing off the earth. We were now 'radio-fingerprinters', or as it was called in Ceylon 'REB-radio elimination of bloodstains' – don't ask why. Clear radio signals from German U-Boats were caught on camera by Wren POs, using cathode-ray oscilloscopes, and transferred to film, producing a wavy or jagged line that looked like an exaggerated ECG trace. We developed the film without using rubber gloves provided at first, until several of us had to go to sickbay with impetigo, which, because we couldn't say what had caused it, was put down to 'sausages'. After developing the film, the first job was to remove the transmitter's carrier wave from the image, by eye and a ruler, and to draw a second trace that had no carrier wave and so was much flatter. Then we compared this with dozens of earlier intercepts, the object being to spot idiosyncracies which would identify the 'signature' of the sender, or a telltale splutter from a specific transmitter. By continuing to monitor messages, and with the help of the D/F boys, U-Boat movements could be followed – very instructive if many were moving in the same direction to form a 'wolf-pack'. On the wall was a huge map of the Atlantic dotted with flags showing where identified U-Boats were. They were EVERYWHERE.

The unnerving cluster of enemy submarines around Spain and the Straits of Gibraltar was very much on my mind when quite unexpectedly Iris and I found ourselves on a draft bound for Ceylon. Of the team of Classifiers originally chosen to go overseas two had dropped out at the last minute. (Wrens under 21 had to get their parents' written permission to go abroad, and this could be revoked). We spent about ten days at Crosby Hall, Chelsea, with draughty nights huddled round a lift-shaft, the presumed safest place in an air-raid. We had more lectures, some on decorum before 'natives', some on 'the tropics' and what to expect. Not getting pregnant was treated obliquely, and we tittered with embarrassment: surely you got married first?

Then one day we marched back to Crosby Hall over Battersea Bridge from a kitting-out warehouse with our tropical uniforms in our arms, topped by monstrous circular white solar topees. There was no attempt at concealment, and if asked the powers-that-be had told us, we were to say we were being drafted to Oban. Everywhere we were being cautioned to 'Be like Dad, keep Mum!' but there were other daunting infringements in practice. At Mill Hill we eight had been given cap ribbons embroidered with the slogan, 'HM Wireless Intelligence' – the phrase stretched right round the cap – but almost before we had sewn these on they were snatched from us and the usual HMS badge substituted. We felt rather let down, especially as Classifiers had no other distinguishing mark: our arm badges were the usual signals' crossed flags. Our future address (which we could tell our parents) would be c/o HMS Lanka, GPO London. My mother told a friend this and she said, "Oh, Lanka's the old name for Ceylon". Maybe the ubiquitous German spies would think this was a double bluff, and would keep a close watch for our white tropical camouflage in snowbound Scotland after all.

SS Stratheden sailed away on 26 February 1944. We Wrens were armed with blanco, Keatings powder, seawater soap, and a balaclava helmet and pair of socks donated by the Canadian Red Cross. Emlyn Williams was the star of an ENSA party going out to India, but watching him skip on deck was the only entertainment the party provided. So we formed a concert party of our own, and Iris, myself and one other sang a song called 'Blond, Brunette and Ginger', in which our efforts to get off with identifiable fellow-passengers were always thwarted by 'a P.O. lurking'. Iris 'Ginger', was ravishingly attractive, and wearing her hair over one eye as a Veronica Lake lookalike was the hit of the show.

We arrived in Bombay on 23 March, having skirted the U-Boats by sailing on a zig-zag course nearly to America. We stayed in Bombay for a couple of weeks, working in the Fleet Mail Office, then on to Colombo in a hot and dirty boat, quite unlike the Stratheden. The battened down dining-room was so stifling that it was impossible to sit there for an entire meal, and there were weevils in the bread. At the first meal Iris gave a little scream when she broke open an appetising bread roll and saw the foreign objects inside; but hunger took over thereafter, and we just shut our eyes and ate.

Bombay and Colombo weren't blacked out! And you could buy oranges and bananas freely! But 'buy' was the snag. In Ceylon Wrens' messing was dictated and I believe the ingredients were actually imported from London, so we had suet pudds, porridge, dried egg and no fruit. It sounds ridiculous, but 'central messing' was the reason we were given. All our pay (now 30 rupees a month) went on lime juice and fruit. The Wrens were scattered in several quarters, ours being St. Peter's Convent, on the Galle Road at Colpetty, a stone's throw from the sea, which was magic. I made friends with a lady who lived in one of the little houses on the narrow path down to the beach. She was hostess to many services people, and here I had my first taste of real Ceylon curries. She was a pianist, and we were encouraged to bring our friends to musical evenings in her tiny sitting room. Later she found someone who lent me a cello, and introduced me to the SWOC orchestra (Services Welfare Organisation of Ceylon ?). The orchestra consisted mainly of Sinhalese, with a handful of Dutchmen, one or two Royal Marines and me, and we had an enthusiastic but diminutive Portuguese conductor. We were an eccentric bunch, with no proper common language, and may have given new meaning to 'entertaining the troops'. We were bussed off to Kandy and Galle to allow them this doubtful privilege, and I took every opportunity for some quick sightseeing before the evening concerts.

The Town Hall, Colombo, where some dances were held for service people, 1945.

At St. Peter's we slept 28 to a dormitory, a bit crowded, but being so near the sea there was always a cool breeze. This was in contrast to our next Wrenery, Kent House in Guildford Crescent, into which several Wrens quarters tipped their occupants at the end of May after a night of torrential monsoon rain. Even when damp and overcast the Crescent looked beautiful – a wide shady road with flowering trees and shrubs; but the ground inside the gate was so thick in mud that we took our white shoes off and squelched to our quarters in bare feet. Here we were some way from the beach, which meant an expedition, rather than just slipping down the road, over the railway line which followed the shoreline, and onto the sand for half an hour.

Kent House was a much larger complex than St. Peter's, with a score of kadjan-roofed Bandas named after ships of the line. Mine was called Defiant, a long Banda with a double cubicle for POs at the end. There were no windows here, only spaces between wall and kadjan roof from which the crows cawed noisily when they weren't drinking from the stagnant puddle below a standpipe in the neglected garden outside. The Bandas were arranged in fours round a central ablution block, each having a paved path to the cold showers and lavatories. There was no hot water and no fixed basins. Instead stone slabs lined a section of the walls, with five or six cold-water taps at intervals along them. The idea was that you could take one of the ten or so tin bowls on the floor underneath the stone slab and fill it with cold water for washing. In practice there was always a dearth of bowls becasuse people filled them with soapy water and left their dirty clothes 'to soak'. I once did likewise with a boyfriend's cricket sweater, forgot it for several weeks, and was then confronted with a child-sized garment stinking to high heaven of rotten eggs. End of boyfriend.

We got used to banging the ends of our slatted beds against the floor and treading on any bedbugs that emerged. (We also got used to the bugs that lived in the majestic cane chairs in the Galle Face and Grand Oriental Hotels. You could always tell a rooky, male or female, by the row of canebug-bites on the backs of his or her legs). Having demolished the bedbugs, we then tucked in the thickest and most airtight mosquito nets I have ever slept under. You could barely see out of them, but they were a necessity, not just against mosquitoes, but against a whole range of exotic flying creatures that divebombed from on high, or scuttled round the floor and climbed the bed legs. Someone once put a thick mug over one of these, and we woke to the scary noise of the mug being trundled across the floor by the Amazon within.

Besides the Bandas there were two kadjan-roofed dining halls, a large one for the majority of us, and a smaller one for CPOs and POs. The officers led a separate existence in the large square colonial house (Kent House itself) beyond the Bandas. Here there were also two recreational rooms, an ironing room and a hairdresser's. The rec rooms were much too small for all the off duty Wrens, which was added incentive to go out with any male who turned up at the Regulating Office by the main gate. And turn up they did. Shortly after we arrived in Ceylon, Admiral Somerville took the salute at a large parade at St. Joseph's Barracks, and in a speech after we had marched around and been inspected he warned us that some of the locals regarded us as 'comforts for the troops', so we mustn't be surprised if rickshaws full of sailors off visiting ships arrived breathlessly, in response to the query, "Master want nice missee?" But I hasten to add that not all our visitors were misinformed, and we were well looked after by our male friends and aquaintances.

Work was at 'HMS Anderson', a one storied complex built on a golf course a few miles from the centre of town. On our first day there we discovered that we couldn't be Classifiers yet because the cathode-ray apparatus hadn't arrived, so we were distributed to the various rooms and told to get on with whatever was going on there. In my case it was room 28, where heads down, everybody smoking, the task in hand was to me the intriguing one of converting a long column of figures into another long column of figures, then looking up the second lot in a Japanese wordlist supplied by the cryptographers and linguists. This was JN25, I discovered, JN being short for 'Japanese Naval', and I revelled in it. I particularly liked corrupt messages, which took ages to decipher, so they tended to get hidden at the bottom of the pile of messages to be decoded. During one night-watch I un-corrupted five of these and my cries of "Eureka" were met with increasingly feeble groans.

The maths necessary for decoding consisted of the ability to add up to nine, so why the Mill Hill people had been so impressed with my school maths (which went a bit higher than that) I have no idea. Perhaps I had wandered into the wrong job. That wasn't impossible! After we had been working in room 28 for about a week, it became apparant that one of the Wrens with us was making heavy weather of the work. Was she SDX? No. A Classifier? No. She had just followed the flow onto the bus on the first day. Suddenly she was packed off back to Kent House: she must have been the only Wren hairdresser ever to have been made to sign the Official Secrets Act.

The messages were brought to us by TWAs, Temporary Women Assistants. They had been recruited locally, and I fear we resented them because they worked only in the daytime, and could take weekdays off and work on Sundays for extra pay. (We on the other hand were on all watches – first day 0800-1200 and 1600-2000, second day 1200-1600 and 2000-0200, third day free, fourth day 0200-0800. This turned "can you come to lunch on Thursday week?" into a mathematical exercise: which watch will I be on?) The TWAs wore nicer uniforms too – and they lived in Colombo's beautiful residential areas, with wonderful gardens and servants. Some even had their own cars, though petrol was almost unobtainable and we ourselves relied on rickshaws, or hitch-hiked on army and navy lorries.

Several months after I became a pseudo-SDX Wren, the Classifiers' section was in business. There were only two of us on each watch, and our room was right at the end of the Anderson complex, beyond the lavatories. It was back to processing yards of film, and charting the progress of Japanese shipping. I had thought my ionospheric skills (such as they were) would never be used, but I was given the unique job of transferring a list of the radio frequencies used by the Japs during the previous month, via some sort of alchemy which I no longer recall, to a graph, which I then took along to the head of the 'Y' section. I can't imagine what it was for, but I hope it helped somebody to do SOMETHING.

Leave came round every three months, and was a great opportunity to see up-country Ceylon. The train took us up through paddy-fields and rubber forests to the lush green hill country. I stayed with three or four different families on the tea-plantations, and thought myself in heaven. The planters and their wives were the most hospitable of folk, and often had a conveyor belt of Wrens, arriving in twos and threes for a wonderful holiday.

Back in Colombo, one the greatest assets to me was the proximity of Merton House, where the Naval Officers and Foreign Office cryptographers and linguists lived. They were only a year or two older than us, and had been wafted away to Bletchley from their university courses. Their ladies' nights were the opportunity for a good meal – no 'central messing' there – and they even gave me an unforgettable 21st birthday party dinner that has gone down in history. On days off we lazed on the beach at Mount Lavinia, eating pineapples after a bathe. We hitch-hiked north to Negombo or south to Kalutara, to swim from a deserted beach – deserted except for the fishermen and their outrigger canoes – and ate huge meals of fried fish and banana fritters in the local resthouses.

In 1996 five of the Merton House crew, and three of us ex-Kent House Wrens, revisited Sri Lanka. We looked in vain for Kent House and Merton House, which had proably disappeared under 'infill' housing. The Chinese restaurants which we had visited so often had gone too: a resident told me that they had packed up almost immediately after the war, when the troops had all left. The waiters in the Galle Face Hotel (where we stayed for a few days in faded slendour) no longer wear tortoiseshell combs in their hair – indeed you cannot buy tortoiseshell as it belongs to an endangered species. Fifty years ago the pavements were besmirched with daubs of betelnut spit, and men's mouths, teeth and tongue were stained bright red from their addiction to it. This is no longer so: the mixture of betelnut, leaves and lime paste was found to be a carcinogen, and chewing it has been banned.

Of course I wasn't sorry to leave. The war was over. Home beckoned, and a new civilian life. But without the Ceylon adventure I would never have formed so many close and enduring friendships, and I have now fulfilled the promise I made to myself to return to the island – one day.

ENID SEAGROVE (nee FEAR) (continued from Chapter 3)

After embarkation leave and a fortnight in Cheyne Walk, Chelsea, having the necessary innoculations and being issued with tropical kit and advice about life in a hot country, I embarked from Liverpool on the 'Empress of Scotland' after an unbelieveably slow train journey from London. I shared a small but comfortable cabin with three other Wrens and had time to settle in well before running into extremely rough conditions round the Bay of Biscay which laid everybody flat. Gradually calm was restored as we entered the Med and we began to enjoy what proved to be a very pleasant three week cruise, with the weather getting hotter and glamorous evenings spent dancing on the Boat Deck. (No shortage of partners due to a surfeit of servicemen aboard). During a short stop at Port Said the locals surrounded the ship in small boats trying to sell their wares and we were hailed by shiploads of servicemen on their way home telling us to 'get yer knees brown!' We sailed on through the Suez Canal watching camels plodding slowly alongside. Crossing the Arabian sea, the first ship not to be blacked-out in that area, we duly arrived in Colombo.

First impressions were of noise, crowds and the unmistakable smell of the East. We transferred to our Quarters in Kent House. Sleeping in large thatched huts, or Bandas, each bunk equipped with a mosquito net, giving a comforting means of escape from the large flying beetles and bugs which invaded the Banda via the gap between wall and roof.

Shortly after arriving in Colombo V.J. Day was celebrated, followed by a grand Victory Parade in the presence of Lord Louis Mountbatten. Eventually ships carrying released prisoners-of-war stopped off briefly in Colombo on their way to the UK. We were called upon to welcome them and provide a meal. They were all very subdued and guant and naturally very anxious to get home.

I worked for part of my six months stay in Colombo in 'HMS Anderson', a signals station, working a normal 8 hour day. I then transferred to the air and rail movements department, again enjoying normal working hours. Leisure time was spent exploring, with frequent visits to surrounding beaches, in particular Mount Lavinia which was one of the locations used in the film 'Bridge on the River Kwai'. I went on leave up-country to Diyatalawa, arriving at the camp in pitch darkness, and in the morning walking out of the hut to find myself in the hills with white clouds scudding below me, a replica of the Shangri-La of Hilton's 'Lost Horizon'.

I transferred to Trincomalee in North-East Ceylon for a brief spell in the S.O.(I).E.I. department, then back to Colombo prior to returning to the UK. Our ship was the 'Arundel Castle'. As we stood silently on deck, our delight to be going home mixed with regret to be leaving the island, I turned round to watch a contingent of RAF personnel coming aboard and came face to face with an old friend from my home town, a cheering sight and we spent a lot of time together on the return voyage.

Quarters were far inferior to those of the outward journey, being located on a very large lower deck with scores of three tier bunks.

Lord Louis Mountbatten, Supreme Allied Commander in S.E. Asia takes the salute. V.J. Day Columbo, 1945. Galle Face Hotel in background.

Colombo, Ceylon. V.J. Day 1945 WRNS march to Royal Marine Band.

I managed to get a top bunk, only to hear after 'Lights-out' the unmistakable scuffle of rat just above my head. Two of us decided to sleep on deck whilst it was warm enough, only to be rudely awakened very early in the mornings by sailors swabbing the decks.

We eventually docked in Southampton and among the large crowd assembled to welcome us was my father. As we were not due to disembark until the following day I managed to get permission to go down the very steep gangplank for a brief re-union with him. As we warmly embraced, cheers and wolf-whistles arose from the decks of the ship. It was a memorable home-coming.

On my return to the UK I remained in the WRNS until marriage in 1948, serving in Chatham Barracks followed by a transfer to the Royal Marine Barracks Chatham.

A few years ago I was asked to give a talk on Bletchley Park. Research via books, articles and documentaries proved to be absorbing and revealing and it was quite a challenge, but very satisfying, to prepare an hour's talk covering the Enigma story. Audiences have quite often produced people who were in some way connected with the Park.

The Bletchley story is an amazing one and although my own input was infinitesimal, I feel very fortunate to have been involved in such an important piece of history.

JOAN RUSSELL (nee HOWARTH)

I was twenty years old, had a sea going father, so was keen to join the WRNS. My difficulty was persuading the Ministry of War Transport to let me go, having achieved that, I was expecting to go into Fleet Maintenance which apart from Cooks and Stewards seemed the only category available in 1942. It was a shock to the system to find I was into some strange thing called Special Duties X, so confidential that it was not to be talked about, etc. I was not the only puzzled girl at Finchley Road College that March day in 1942.

It was a nervous bunch who arrived at Bletchley Park some weeks later – quite a few things were strange, Crawley Grange our first home had two bathrooms which we found could accommodate at least three girls, if not four at a time after mid-night watch – one in the bath, one standing wielding the hand shower and one at the basin with one ready to be next. Cooking facilities were primitive, I remember Cooks saying, "Well, which do you want? Cheese surprise or a cup of tea, the stove will not do both". There was much discussion about whether the Oak Room was haunted; stories about a bricked up baby in years past were trotted out from time to time. We also had a funny happening when an RAF Officer from the nearby 'drome was too tiddly to find his way home from the village pub and wandered in and fell asleep on one of the beds (pardon me, bunks) in "Nelson cabin". Unfortunately, the occupants were all new girls coming off duty at mid-night watch for the first time and were worried about reporting it in case it was 'The Norm'!

I moved to Wavendon House and there we entertained our first Americans. The Duke of Kent had been killed and plunged the Air Force into Official Mourning, we unfortunately had planned our very first dance and suddenly, no partners. One very enterprising girl rang the Telephone Exchange and asked if there were any other officers in the vicinity and struck oil, the Americans had just arrived at Thurleigh. Suggesting forty five men, they suggested two hundred! We had our first view of Jeeps, the convoy did not bother to use the drive but drove straight over the fields!

Unfortunately, the mortality rate among the airmen was high but we established a pleasant rapport with a few and they used to put their cycles on the train at Bedford and then cycle up from the village to spend an hour or two chatting in the F'castle.

One evening there was an urgent summons from the village to go down and identify two men picked up by the local Home Guard as suspicious characters. Evidently the pink pants, olive coats, etc. of the Americans plus Southern voices had been enough to arouse the local men and two very frightened airmen were identified.

From Wavendon I went as part of the first sixteen SDX Wrens to Kenya. Once again our non identification proved difficult. On the ship I was nailed by a Commander who asked, "What do you do?" Quick thinking Joan, I said, "I am a writer", the first thing that came into my mind. "Fine" he said, "I have work for you". I then looked blank and had to admit I was not a writer. "What do you do then?" I said, "Special Duties". "Well what on earth is that?" Having then been told I could not tell him, he obviously thought he was dealing with an idiot and marched off. Life would have been much easier for us if a badge of some sort had been designed and some sort of credible story so that we could all say the same thing.

From Mombasa I went to Egypt on three months leave to be married. I was engaged to an Australian Airman before I joined the WRNS and he was stationed in the Middle East. Fortunately he met one of my Wren friends in Alexandria, one of the few non SDX I knew. She was a coder and we had been at Finchley together. She told him where I was and he saw our Superintendent Nile, Miss Frith and I saw the Naval Captain where we worked in Mombasa and one way and another I was given leave. I went up on an old coal burner cargo ship with a crowd of Dock-yard workers wives being returned from South Africa, two other Wrens and four Australian Navy men. These together with a number of Shell wives and children who were en route to join husbands, etc. We had an eventful trip, breaking down in the Red Sea, not to be recommended, masses of children and only the hatch tops for them to play on, we were always rescuing some adventurous child from a deck railing or worse.

After being married in Alexandria I knew I was supposed to return to Colombo where Eastern Fleet had moved. Usual Navy though, when I imparted this knowledge I was smartly told I could not possibly know that and would be sent back to Mombasa. The fact that I knew there was no-one there made no difference. After arriving in Mombasa there was the difficulty of getting me to Ceylon. Eventually there were now three of us awaiting trans-shipment, we had an interview with a Welsh Merchant Captain who would not take us without meeting us to see if he approved because he did not like women on his ship in wartime. The fact that my father was in peacetime a Chief Engineer in the Merchant Navy seemed sufficient reference and we set sail. We travelled with some white officers and a few hundred Askaris. No lifeboats only Carley floats. The Askaris used to sit on the deck outside our cabin and discuss how many wives their improved army money would allow them to buy.

I spent two years in Colombo – one episode bears telling. The American Consul and then the Vice Consuls were very friendly with some of us and on one occasion they had a formal dinner party for one of their visiting Generals. We of course had the usual system of passes, etc., we also had a system whereby our sentries woke us to go on duty at mid-night by knocking on the Banda door and holding up a lamp and waited while we signed the book. Well, during a lull in the conversation my escort to the dinner enquired how I was going for time. I answered, "Oh do not worry, I have signed the knocking up book". Of course to an American it meant something completely different and I wondered why I was the centre of a number of pairs of eyes all of a sudden. Confusion all round, not least me!

We also had the occasion when one of the visiting aircraft carriers caused some confusion. We had a system overseas of only being allowed out with an escort at night (darkness fell at six pm), plus signing a book to say where we were going and with whom. Well this must have become a little garbled with the telling because I came off duty one day to see our sentries slam the big gate behind me. I looked up the road and there must have been most of the ships company off duty from the carrier coming up the road. Fascinated, I stood by the Regulating Office to hear what went on. Our two sentries were confronting this sea of Gobs (American sailors) and it seemed to consist of demands. "We wanna Wren", "Well you can't have one", etc. It seemed because of our little signing methods the word had gone round that if you wanted a Wren you signed for one like a parcel and she was presumably supposed to be handed over like a parcel. I disappeared quickly leaving our poor two sentries to deal with masses of very disgruntled Gobs.

Finally, when I was leaving Ceylon for home the American Vice Consuls gave me a farewell party. During the evening which was a great success I could not understand why first one Vice Consul and then another kept looking under cushions and chairs in odd moments. Next day came the explanation; they had ordered a bag of live crabs to be cooked for the party and some had escaped and they were worried in case a guest was suddenly going to encounter one or worse still, sit on one!

Joan concludes "All in all my time in the WRNS was an enjoyable experience in many ways, frustrating like all Service life I imagine, in others. Like many people I have been back to a number of the places, Bletchley Park, Crawley Grange, Wavendon House, Mombasa, Egypt, South Africa, etc.; little remains to show where we all spent so much time.

Life in Australia has been great fun and I do meet Wrens here on the coast from time to time and have one close friend who served in Malta and married an Airman too. As a matter of interest five girls who married Australians did a broadcast for the ABC

(Australian Broadcasting Company).

DOROTHY SMITH (nee ROBINSON)
(Continued from Chapter 3)

After two months at BP, we were sent to Crosby Hall, Cheyne Walk, London – that is, first we had embarkation leave, all very exciting. While at Crosby Hall, our time was filled in for us with visits of interest in London, and from day to day we never knew when we would be off – or how. After about two weeks, the great news came that we must not go out, as in a few hours we were to leave London – having no idea how or where. We joined a troop train somewhere outside London and started a long overnight journey, none of us knowing where we were headed for, until the next morning, I recognised the area, we were in Renfrewshire where I had gone to boarding school! (None of the girls with me knew it, as they were English, so I was able to tell them). Of course, our troopship and convoy were anchored at Clydebank, and there we boarded the huge S.S. Strathaird for our journey to the East at last.

As it was now March, the weather was very windy and wet and the first week or so we had quite a rough passage out into the Atlantic. Years later someone told me that we had gone halfway to America, but with wartime security, no one was allowed to know anything. The ships in the convoy always seemed far away and I know that we must have had several submarine scares, as we often zig-zagged on route, but life was so exciting and there were only about 100 girls on board, (60 Wrens and 40 Queen Alexandria nurses), with some 5-6000 servicemen, so we really had a marvellous time. The OC/Troops had to 'ration' the men daily to meet us, so we had different batches up on B-deck every day, with dancing on deck at night. Lights out was early – around 10pm or so. Being a P/O, I was in charge, with another P/O (Anne Robson) of a cabin D/28, of 28 Wrens in double-decker bunks, and we had a lot of fun.

I remember seeing the Rock of Gibraltar and telling a young ship's officer that I was glad that at last we were out of the huge Atlantic with its submarines – whereupon he replied that the Mediterranean, just newly opened again, would be much more hazardous, as we could very easily be divebombed by the Germans from Crete! As it happened we had an air alert in that area, but all was well.

One of my clearest recollections is that of waiting in our ship and convoy to enter the Suez Canal. It was gloriously hot and sunny and the sea had that smooth greenish tinge all around. We were up on B-deck with lots of the lads, looking over the side watching ship movements and generally wondering what was going to happen next.... when we began to notice that a lot of landing craft seemed to be moving towards us, filled with men in white helmets. I shall never forget as they came alongside, far below, one helmet looked upwards at us on deck and emitted a loud cry, "Gee DAMES!" Whereupon the whole flotilla of landing craft looked up and bawled, "Gee! DAMES!" – We girls simply fled down to our cabins and locked ourselves in.... In subsequent days, the Yanks were rationed to meet us, like all the other troops, but somehow or other they seemed to appear here and there on our deck in spite of this, and I must say, they were often very amusing, and of course terrible flirts. Our British lads were absolutely furious and used to surround us, 3 or 5 to one Wren, as an anti-Yank bodyguard, whenever they could, from then onwards. We also had a contingent of ANZACS on board at Suez, on their way home after fighting in North Africa. The New Zealanders were more polite than the Aussies, and they were all very friendly and surprised to see women on the troopship. One of the Australians, a young redhead soldier from Adelaide, took a fancy to me and became a real pest from then till we disembarked at Bombay, but I was sorry for him as he was a young lad and had had a very serious wound in North Africa. His older mates tended to look after him. He wanted me to marry him in Bombay.... nothing was further from my mind!!!

Sometimes the Maoris would come up on deck in the evening and sing to us, squatting around in a circle, humming and strumming as the sun went down in the Red Sea – very beautiful – their song "Now is the Hour", and I remember sailing slowly through the Suez Canal, it seemed as if we'd touch the sides of it in our huge liner, and the British soldiers stationed along the empty banks, all shouting up at us "You're going the wrong way!" It all became very nostalgic for me, as I had sailed home from India as a little girl of four with my mother and sister some 18 years before, all of which seemed an eternity to me at the time, a whole lifetime in fact, and everything about it was like a dream come true as I had wanted to go back again all my short life.

Aden, then into the Arabian sea – calm and smooth and greenish-blue. My "Mecca" had been Bombay, and we were to disembark there in a few days time.... I could hardly believe it. But one day before Bombay, on a sizzling hot afternoon while we were up on deck, we started to zig-zag violently and word got around that a Japanese submarine was chasing us. Nasty, but all was well. And then the far coastline of India, and a very young ship's officer told me that the hill I could see was Malabar Hill, Bombay where I had lived with my family as an infant and the name of which was like magic in my family at home, and now we were gently sailing into the harbour.... I was truly back. There was the huge and impressive building of the Taj Mahal Hotel, and the Gateway to India, an arch built by the British to commemorate the visit of King George V and Queen Mary in 1911.... Eventually we piled down the gangway, to be met by 'local' Wrens who laughed at us in our brand new spotless white topees, which they said we'd never wear again – and we never did. Shame as they really did something for one, and what a waste of Admiralty money!

Being in transit, we were stationed at a large bungalow in Bombay called Vasanji, in Nepean Sea Road, which had been the Japanese Embassy before the war. It was SO hot but we loved it all – the palm trees, the calls of the chipmunks and the screeching birds early in the mornings, the FRUIT, especially oranges and bananas, which none of us had seen for years, and then the truly wonderful shopping in Bombay, where no coupons were needed. Oh the joy of it! After wartime, blackout, spartan, cold battered Britain, this was just fantastic. It was HOT, we could buy food and materials without restriction in shops or in exciting Crawford Market, everything was colourful and noisy and with no blackout, lights blazed all evening from streetlamps, houses, hovels, shops. It was BLISS! We used to say we'd tell our grandchildren about the whole experience – and so we do. We drove around in cheap and very ramshackle taxis or in horse-drawn gharis, often with boyfriends from the ship; we danced at the marvellous Green's Restaurant overlooking the bay, and I visited my parents successors in their gorgeous Bank house up on Malabar Hill. Months later, when I received a reply from my parents, telling them about all this, I think they were almost as thrilled about it as I was. We never knew from day to day how long we'd be in transit in Bombay; It turned out to be two weeks – and what a two weeks! One evening I was invited to have dinner in my parents' Bank house – that is the one up on Malabar Hill, with its lovely garden, tennis court, etc. overlooking the bay, Marine Drive, known as "The Queens necklace", as it twinkled in a beautiful circle of lights at night. Imagine my horror when I spied three of the ANZACs I'd known on the ship, walking up the drive towards the house! My hostess Mrs Drake, was embarrassed but marvellous, asking them to come in for a drink and a game of billiards.... It turned out that 'Blue' the one who liked me, heard where I had gone, so he and his friends followed in a taxi. All very embarrassing as I could see both sides – many of the British in India had very little idea that there was a war on, and the servicemen had had a ghastly time in North Africa, so why should they not be welcomed with open arms everywhere? Furthermore, non-commissioned ranks were barred from all the good British Clubs in India, a very sore point with the troops, and rightly so. All very tricky.

After some two weeks of glorious fun in Bombay, we left the huge Victoria Railway Terminal in Bombay, an incredible Victorian Gothic edifice modelled on our Imperial Science Museum, joining a troop train to journey south to Ceylon. The squalor of poor Indians in the station was indescribable; some destitutes live all their lives on platforms, all very pathetic. Soon we were out in the country, rolling open and parched. Four of us good friends, P/Os (Anne Robson, Eiken Bonner Thomas, Chris North and I) shared a compartment on this amazing, long, tedious, scorching train journey, when the dry heat burnt up our lips, throats, clothes, and we had to keep all the windows open day and night just to get air – the air itself hot, dusty and burning. No fans or airconditioners then! When eventually I wrote telling my parents of this and weeks later, received their reply, my father in Scotland, remembering his years in India, wrote: "No white woman could have endured such conditions in the hot season in India"....!! Crossing the Deccan in April, everything seemed burnt black – the people, the ground, which was also heavily cracked for miles, the cattle – everything. Our train used to stop for meals at stations, when swarms of beggars would come alongside the windows, some showing the most appalling sores, begging for alms. We had to get off and sit in the platform restaurants for our breakfast, lunch and supper, which always seemed to consist of bacon and eggs, chicken and chicken. We had lots of laughs of course, and the whole squalid trip (no washing water available, or the minimum), was a tremendous adventure. At, or near Bangalore, we had to change trains which involved moving all the luggage too, and we four were put in charge of the luggage for 60 Wrens – quite a responsibility, especially when porters tall and small, all Indian grabbed as much as they could possibly carry and rushed off, heaven knew where. One or two porters could carry five or six suitcases – two on the head, two under the arms and one in each hand! Somehow, miraculously, we found all the luggage in the right place for the new train – what a relief.

And so on and on we rumbled, unable to sleep at nights for the intense heat and by now very uncomfortable indeed in our dry, dusty, blue cotton uniforms (bluettes). At last we reached the southern tip of India and embarked on an old ferryboat to take us across the Gulf of Mannar to Ceylon. I think this trip took about 24 hours; anyway by now we were so hot, sticky, dirty and uncomfortable, we longed to wash and change, but not much chance of that, with water rationed morning and evening about one hour on each time for so many of us. A train was waiting for us on disembarkation before dawn, in the north of Ceylon. Suddenly we were in steaming, hot tropical rain forest, so refreshing and exotic after the intense dry heat of India, and I remember standing in the corridor of the train with Anne, all feelings of exhaustion forgotten, watching this gorgeous lush greenery whizzing by – we were so excited.

In Colombo we were stationed at Kent House in Flower Road. It had been a large house privately owned before the war and now the compound was filled with lots of whitewashed huts (cadjan huts) with thatched roofs, which provided sleeping quarters for up to 500 Wrens. The big house was the mess: concrete paths lead from it to all the huts, so that one had dryish feet in the heavy rains, we discovered. Alongside the paths were lines of brilliant zinnias and I remember how beautiful they looked at night under the lights along the paths. Our work was done some miles away in the jungle at HMS Anderson W/T and as ever we worked in naval watches or shifts around the clock. When going on duty we had to congregate under a huge banyan tree in the compound where two or three naval buses (trucks) waited to take us the few miles out to Anderson. Our drivers were locals and pretty rum characters too; one, Robert, a skinny, scruffy chap, used to take a swig of his arak bottle before revving up and driving us, one toe on the gas, hurtling through the jungle.... we often wondered if he'd arrange to take his busload of white women down to the Pettah (Bazaar) instead and sell us!! But everything in those days was a big laugh, so we didn't worry. We did have one, just one little naval rating to 'guard' us in each duty transport, though I doubt if he'd have been much use in a crisis.

On watch, we P/Os shared a room/hut with several others – three Admiralty civilians, Commander Marshall and two Malays, Omar and Hashim, with whom he had escaped from Singapore, probably on a raft, no time before. We received our traffic (signals) by messenger from the big W/T watchroom, but while we never saw the inside of it, they never saw our workroom either. We had all, no doubt, signed the Official Secrets Act, and no one ever discussed his or her work with anyone else.

In Kent House, at first we were put up in long bandas, our beds being wooden slatted so very hard, and our mattresses wet through as it was the rainy season and there had been some trouble. We didn't really mind as it was always warm, especially under our khaki mosquito nets. Our kit was stacked under our bed and I well remember one's shoes, belts, bags, etc. anything made of leather, being thick with hairy mildew after three or four days if not polished. The smell too!.... Food, incredibly, was exactly the same in Ceylon as it was in UK – Navy Victuals provided hot Spotted Dick pudding even in the stifling humid heat! There was an excellent canteen in the town, run by local lady volunteers, and here we would get lovely bowls of local fruit salads and so on, which we never saw in Wren Quarters.

Most of us tried to join the Colombo Swimming Club for which there was a long waiting list, and many a pleasant hour was spent there while we were off duty. The Admiralty amazed us by suggesting that those of us who owned bicycles could have them shipped out from the UK – and so they were, though of course, it took weeks for them to arrive. My father thought this fantastic and had my beautiful Raleigh crated up for the trip; it duly arrived and was a great joy to me in Colombo, everything being very flat there. It also meant that in daytime, one was not obliged to take a rickshaw when going out. These were man-pulled and though a most comfortable ride, the rickshaw coolies were a very poor, tough lot and could be most unpleasant if they considered one's tip too small; we girls were on service pay! They used to curse and spit beetelnut just too close to one's feet, and there was the odd tale of a Wren being tipped up backwards and robbed.

There were always plenty of dances at Service messes, so we went out most evenings when not on duty – that is, until we realised we just could not keep it up any longer, and became more selective. Romances too, of course and my first real one hit me a few months after we arrived, but the Sub.Lt. RNVR seconded to the Indian Navy had to go back to his landing craft unit in Bombay and it all really faded out.... The favourite evening spot was the little nightclub, "The Silver Fawn", where we'd be taken for a really glamourous evening's dinner dancing, the live band playing dance favourites, the lights low, flowers for one's dress, gorgeous food – it was incredibly heady stuff for girls of our age (early 20s) – and there was usually the knowledge that the boy friend would be leaving for Burma or India soon, never to return. After all, there was a war on.... As there were literally about 1,000 men to 1 girl, and many of the lads had not seen a white girl for months or years, you can imagine how spoilt we were. We loved it! How different and how naive we were in those days; one never heard of any misbehaviour and we knew if any occurred, we'd be sent straight back to Britain, (I only heard of one case who was); there seemed to be a sort of protection and we all had been brought up so much more strictly than the young nowadays, knowing what was right and what was wrong, with no shades in between!

Ceylon, (now Sri Lanka) is the most beautiful exotic island, having three monsoons every year, so very green and lush, hot and humid, a few degrees north of the equator. We had few opportunities to see the island, but most of us managed to spend our annual leaves on tea estates upcountry with planters whose hospitality to service personnel was tremendous. No doubt they felt it was part of their war effort, but we enjoyed it too. I used to go to stay with friends of my parents on tea or rubber estates, taking a Wren friend with me. The planters led notoriously lonely lives and seemed to enjoy the young company as well as hearing about the war at home up till the time we had left the UK. In many ways, the war hadn't really touched them and I shall always remember going to the weekly social with our hosts, Mr and Mrs Hugh Gordon of Bogawatalawa (a tea estate cut out of the jungle by Mr Gordon's father or grandfather); this consisted of tennis at the little local club, tea and then a cinema show country style –

the seats were club chairs and our bare legs got bitten by 'putchies' in the cane seats! We saw the film "The Gentle Sex" with Leslie Howard in the lead, about British Servicewomen (ATS) transport-driving during the war. It was excellent, but we were amused that our host, Mr Hugh Gordon could not believe that women could do such jobs and Anne and I had to try to convince him that this was true. They really had no idea.... Back in Colombo, life was hectic enough and I doubt if we watchkeepers ever got enough sleep. The social life was overwhelming and we of course thoroughly enjoyed it. As if we hadn't enough dates, once a Yankee Naval Task Force arrived in Colombo and we were all detailed off by Chief Officer to attend some of their dances, either on board ship or in the Town Hall. This was unpopular, as we felt that the Yankees were just too fresh and as none of them had seen 'Dames' for a very long time, we were rather nervous. Even when shopping in the Fort in the centre of Colombo, they would approach one in rows of 8 or 10 and encircle one – help! For the week or so that they were in harbour, we tried to stay in quarters but even then there was a continuous crowd of them waiting at the regulating office at the gate of Kent House, bawling, "We want DAMES – we want Dames!" Ghastly. When I was on regulating duty there one evening, American boys would manage to trickle through the gates occasionally, through our thin naval guard, and I remember two of them, nice lads, sidling up to my desk and saying, "Is Mary in? Is Mary in?" To which I'd reply, "We have 500 Wrens here. Which Mary do you want?" Their reply: "Oh, any Mary will do...." You had to laugh, but they didn't get away with Mary....

Sometimes we would go on board an aircraft carrier – I remember 'Illustrious' – to a dance, when we danced in the hangar to two wonderful bands and had to hop over the squares marked out on the deck. The men used to cut in as we danced, and I recall starting a sentence with one partner and having about four different partners before I finished it. These service dances were never as much fun as the personal dates at the beloved Silver Fawn or at the old Mount Lavinia Hotel by the sea, when one dressed up in evening dress and waiters served a beautiful meal to the throbbing dance music.

Before my arrival in Ceylon, my elder brother, Alistair, had been in India with the army for two years and having volunteered for the Chindits, was now in Burma. What fun it would be if somehow we could meet on leave.... Letters to and from Burma were erratic, to say the least, but eventually he told me he would be able, with luck, to meet me – if I could get transport up to India. My Chief Officer listened sympathetically to my request; one had to have real compassionate grounds in those days for any such thing – and after much on/offing over the months, it was arranged that I could fly up to stay with my parents successors in the Mercantile Bank House in Bombay for the coming Christmas (1944), my leave being some ten days. Naturally, my hostess had to write to Chief Officer inviting me and replies had to be received, all of which took weeks. At last I was off – on my very first flight – WHAT a thrill! From RAF Ratmalana, some twelve of us passengers took off in a Dakota, all grey paint, no upholstery, nuts and bolts and metal all around. I shall never forget the wonderful experience of taking off and rising slowly up, up till suddenly we were alongside a CLOUD and our wing 'touched it'! Terrific! As I was the only female on the flight I was given special treatment, in spite of the fact that there were two or three 'Red Tabs' (very Senior Army ranks) on board. No food in flight, so we landed a few hours later in Southern India at RAF Cochin. The RAF lads who received us took us across the runway to a tiny wooden shed outside which hung a pub-type sign "Ye Olde Coach Inne". Inside the hut we sat down for tea and brilliantly coloured iced cakes – much loved by the Indians. Then up and off again, and not for one second was I bored – there was the earth far below and nearby were clouds and I was on my way, back to my beloved Bombay which had so many associations with my early childhood. After a flight of some 7½ hours in all (it would now take three or less) we arrived at Santa Cruz Airport, Bombay. The hot dry air burned one's face on leaving the aircraft; I noticed it forcibly after the intense humidity of Colombo.

The Bank bungalow, a palatial affair with gorgeous views over Bombay and the long sweep of the marina below, was a wonderful place to stay in, with its lovely garden and tennis court, and I longed to be able to describe it to my parents who had left it some years before. When eventually they got my letters about it all, they were thrilled. My brother arrived next day and I still remember our meeting in the front hall, after over three years of war. Three other friends of his had also come down from Burma on leave, so for the next ten days I was swept off my feet by these super chaps – none of whom had seen a white girl for years – and I was very spoiled. We swam at the pool at Breach Candy, danced at the Taj Mahal hotel (I wore a white evening dress and asked THEM to dance with me), ate, drank, went rides all over town in horse drawn gharis, and so on. It was absolutely wonderful. I never seemed to have enough sleep as we were burning the candle at all ends, so before ten days were up I really began to feel a wreck but didn't tell.... How I hated having to leave and say goodbye! But I had promised faithfully to come back on time, no matter what the temptation, and it certainly was tempting. So, farewell to my brother, who had to return soon to Burma and some of the heaviest fighting, and to my India. I vowed to return one day.... As we flew down over Ceylon and the airport at Ratmalana, I knew that one of the biggest thrills of my life was ending (I had just had my 23rd birthday). We touched the tarmac and as we did so it seemed very bumpy indeed, until at last the Dakota came to a halt. The air ground staff who met us at the bottom of the steps said we had a burst tyre. All I could think of as we taxied in, jolting forwards and backwards heavily, was that in front of me on the pilot's door was a notice "Crew Only", and I remember thinking that whatever happened, I must not get thrown in there! Extraordinary how one's mind works in an emergency.

Of course I was immensely grateful to my Chief Officer for arranging my flight to India to meet my brother, but it was not for a long time that it dawned on me that no doubt this was because nobody knew in those days who would survive the fighting and who would not, and here was a chance at least of our meeting once again. My brother did, happily, come through it all and we always looked back on our "Christmas 1944" holiday in Bombay as one of the happiest we had ever had.

Lord Louis Mountbatten first had his HQ at Kandy but in 1945 he moved up to Delhi. When in Ceylon, he occasionally came down to give us Wrens a peptalk, and he was so handsome in his tropical whites, shorts, thick 'scrambled eggs' on his hat and epaullettes, that we all swooned. He knew this of course, and enjoyed it. Friends who were Wrens at Kandy told us that he always had himself photographed while driving his jeep, from a certain low position in the drive up to HQ in the Peradinaya Gardens, so that he would look extra tough and handsome!

The only time I saw him actually at Kandy was at the end of the war when I got a lift in a crowded naval truck up there to see the annual Perahera Festival in August 1945. Sixty elephants of all sizes took part in a moonlight procession all through the little town, electric lights of all colours twinkling from their heads, bejewelled cloths draped all over their backs and lots of Kandyan dancers in brilliant robes and silver headdressses, twirling torches, dancing in between them.

Lord Mountbatten and his party in their gleaming white uniforms sat on a dais outside the old Queen's Hotel, while we mingled with the crowds. The Tooth of the Buddha which is said to be kept in a sacred casket in the Temple of the Tooth beside the lake at Kandy, is carried in a jewelled casket on top of the grandest elephant for three successive nights round Kandy by the light of the moon. Unforgettable.

Around VJ-Day in August 1945, a few of us managed to get up to Trincomalee, the huge naval base in the north of Ceylon, for several days. The excitement was enormous, for now the war was over and we had won.... We lived in a Wren bungalow on the beach; on VJ night, some naval officers called for us in a DUKW (amphibious sort of tank that could go forwards and backwards almost anywhere) up into the hills overlooking Trinco, to see the Fleet 'dressed overall' – what a sight. No doubt all the hooters were hooting too, I can't remember, but it was such fun and we were all thrilled to bits.

Now our particlar job was finished, as no more Japanese signals were forthcoming, and time hung on our hands. Before long however, we were enlisted to help in probably the most satisfying and at the same time, moving work I have ever taken part in – the reception of prisoners of war from the Far East, as they sailed in shiploads, perhaps one or two a week, through Colombo on their way home to Britain. Lady Moore, wife of the Governor General of Ceylon organised us through the Red Cross into groups, most of which received the ex-POWs in army trucks from their ships, to the Echelon Barracks in Colombo. Prisoners who were too ill to come ashore stayed on board ship and groups of Wrens went onboard to see and help them there. Some of these patients were almost blind from malnutrition in the camps, and one of my friends told me that as they walked among them, the POWs in their bunks did not even see them. A doctor told us that their sight would recover with adequate vitamins. Among others I worked in Echelon Barracks in a mock up Post Office hut, where three of us sorted mail for any incoming ex-POWs and helped any of them who wanted to send a message home. It was hard to remain dry-eyed when a lad would open and read the first letter he had had from home – a mother, wife or sweetheart – for several years. One chap read out to me, "She says 'I am still waiting' " as he broke down and wept. During the one day that they spent ashore, they were kitted-up, fed with a very light salad meal and only half a glass of beer (they were too unused to it to be able to drink more), given UK papers to read – some asked straight away, "Have you got the News of the World?" – and helped to send messages home. There were civilians too, some looking very emanciated indeed and it was a fact that the services with their cameraderie stood up to camp conditions better than individual civilians. Thin, fragile-looking gentlemen, no doubt much younger than they seemed, trailed about in jungle-made slippers and hats, and were touchingly grateful and polite to us for the slightest help we were only too glad to give them. The civilian women were taken to a 'make-up' hut where they had showers and hairdos and were made up; it was all so good for their morale but to see their worn and gaunt faces underneath was sad. We were very moved by it all and felt humble in the presence of the ex-POWs who had suffered so much for so long. They on their part, told us how thrilled they were to see white women, as most of them had embarked straight from the prison camps, and Colombo was their first sight of the free world after all those years. Lists of the passengers on these ships would be posted up a few days before they came in and we would scan them to see if anyone whom we knew, or knew of, might be on board. I met quite a few servicemen whom I knew of, some friends of my family, several of whom were doctors, and I know from them that their surprise at meeting anyone they might know there in Colombo was as great as my own. I still have two letters written by two young doctors soon afterwards and posted in the Middle East at their next port of call, describing the wonder of it all. WE felt the privileged ones.... One heard from some of the soldiers how the doctors had performed operations in the camps with the lid of sardine tins – and so on. I sent a cable home to my parents, asking them to phone the father of a young ex-POW in our hometown, to say that I had met his son and that he was safe and well and en route home. Great rejoicing. And overall there was this touching gratitude on their part – after all they had been through.

Several of us in Special Duties wanted to stay out East after the war had ended, so we went to Chief Officer to ask if we could do so, or go on to Singapore. We were very disappointed when she said this was not possible as there was no job for us to do, alas. We had had such a wonderful time in Ceylon and did not relish the return to poor old grey, cold Britain immediately after the war. One had to wait now for one's number of demobilisation to come up, to be shipped home. In November, 1945, my date fell due and I really was sad, all the more so as not one of my own special group was on the same draft – on the "SS Strathnaver". So finally the day arrived and some 300 (I think) Wrens embarked. As we sailed out of Colombo harbour late in the afternoon, I stood alone at the stern of the ship, the tears rolling down my cheeks.... and I wondered how long it would be till I could go East again. (Little did I guess that I was to marry in 1956 and spend 18 years in tropical Africa, although India and Ceylon always took first place for me).

Conditions going home were actually far worse than those we had when sailing out; now we 300 Wrens were all packed into one enormous deck space in triple-decker bunks, all the luggage for three to be stacked under the bottom bunk! Water was turned on only a few hours a day, so life was not too luxurious.... I longed to see places on route like Suez, but of course this was out of the question, troops never having shore leave, but I promised myself to return one day. (This my husband and I did in 1989, to India, but of course we flew over most of the places en route to a most wonderful holiday all over India, 44 years later.... The old magic was still there, the colour, the mystery, the romance, the incredible arts and crafts, the history.... and always, the charm and friendliness).

As we sailed home, the weather naturally got colder and stormier; it was the end of November after all, and we felt the sudden drop in temperature acutely. It was windy and cold and wet when finally we arrived at Southampton and disembarked from the "Strathnaver" and joined a train to take us to Waterloo Station. We had heard that there was a dock strike in progress (or porter strike?), anyway, at Waterloo we had to find huge trollies and load all our WRNS luggage on to them. No help was given by the troops – they unchivalrously mocked us, saying that as we had been too grand to go out with them in the Far East, we could jolly well get on with it now! We laughed and got on with it alright and soon all the baggage was in the WRNS lorries which had met us to take us in our separate directions to different Wren establishments for demobilisation. (The fact was that in the Far East, with 1000 men to a girl, it was quite impossible for us all to meet all the men!) And so I was soon home again in the north of Scotland, to face one of the coldest winters ever.... but my parents being ex-India people themselves, were very understanding.

Life in Britain immediately after the war was really grey and one felt sorry for those who had not had any of the fun and colour and excitement that we had had. There were inumerable shortages and ration cards for food and clothing were to continue for some time yet. People had had a hard, cheerless time but the fact that we had won, incredibly, this six-year war when at times it seemed impossible – a true David and Goliath story – was everything. And of course, the spirit of patriotism was immensely strong; Winston Churchill was everyone's hero, not only in Britain but in Europe and overseas and there was a big question for most of us young people: "Where do we go from here?" After all the one-track-mindedness of the war years, when everything and everyone had one purpose – Victory – it was very hard to readjust one's thinking and, partly no doubt, through exhaustion both nationwide and individually, to decide what to do now. Those of us who had no special training (I only had an MA degree), felt lost and missed the direction and friendships of service life. The saying, "I couldn't care less" crept into everything; a negative attitude, but for a time understandable.

I finally decided to take a course in dress design/pattern cutting, which my sister, now married, had taken up before the war in London. It was in London that I met my future husband, on leave from Nigeria, West Africa, and early in 1956 I sailed out to Lagos, Nigeria to be married. Back to the tropics, like Ceylon only a few degrees north of the equator, extremely hot and humid, but colourful – this time to Africa where I was to spend, with annual leaves home by air, 18 years. Again, the friends, the social life, the parties, palmbeaches, flowers, heat, travel, interesting people of all colours and occupations.... I would not have missed any of it and know that I have been very fortunate to have had such an interesting and full life. I have two grown-up daughters and I often tell them that if there had to be a war, I am glad I was in it especially in the WRNS.

DAPHNE JENKINS (nee POOLE)

Daphne was a Typex Wren at HMS Anderson, Colombo, quartered in Kent House. She had begun her WRNS career in Mill Hill Training Depot for just one week before being sent to Greenwich Naval College for a teleprinter course. In 1943 she was sent to Mombasa, East Africa, where the Wrens came under the command of COISEF (Chief of Intelligence Staff Eastern Fleet). From there they were sent to Colombo to join HMS Anderson. The group of eight girls managed to stay together despite moves to accommodate them in different bandas according to watches.

Daphne writes, "Our address in Colombo continued to be COISEF and we only became HMS Anderson some time after we began operation there. Before that there was no Anderson, hence my feeling it to be wrong to refer to it as "an outpost of Bletchley Park". We had a circuit (BRUSA) in operation which included Melbourne, Pearl Harbour and Washington, none of whom, I think, would like to be called outposts. Later as the war progressed, Guam and Wake Island came in. The whole constituted a big loop with everyone passing their traffic to the next in line".

"At the time of arrival in Mombasa there were only two Typex machines operating. The move to Colombo was in two main parties, enabling one to remain to continue the monitoring of Japanese radio until the first party set up shop in Colombo. The second party then followed and the rear party, of course, was on the ill-fated Khedive Ismail. (Our ship was torpedoed the day before we were to embark and we were bundled on board HMS Chitral, an armed merchant cruiser, instead, with instructions to expect ad hoc accommodation. It was. Wrens lined the sides as we left harbour, cheered by HM ships as we passed)".

"At first the Typex Wrens were the only ones to keep night watch. What a trial that was. Not many people were around at night, mainly the Radio Receiving Room, all male and no facilities of any description".

The Typex section they worked in was near some GCCS people, who when they had a knotty problem in trying to beat the American code-breakers in solving a coded message, asked the Typex people to try to keep the noise down (a near impossibility) and allow them to concentrate.

Daphne continues, "After acquisition of the American CCMs (Combined Cypher Machines) we moved to a big specially built air-conditioned room near the big Radio Room, where the noise rose about tenfold. Unlike human beings, if machinery did not like the temperature it just stopped working, hence the air-conditioned room". Daphne remembers a wandering Chief Officer who came for a look-see, asking how they could possibly hear one another. She was told they talked through it. Daphne had to demonstrate the machinery a few times to Generals, Air Vice Marshals, etc. and even had a little tete-a-tete with Admiral Fraser, but missed seeing Mountbatten.

"The symbols taken down by the WTs (Wireless Telegraphists) were translated to Japanese kanas which we then coded for transmission to the next station in line which was Melbourne. Our incoming traffic for decoding consisted of signals from GCCS and on the CCMs we worked straight off High Speed Automatic Morse tapes. For interest at the peak of operations one day, I counted 33 machines, roughly half and half Typex and CCMs, 30 in the watch, (4 of them Naval Tels) and 16 codes, American, British and Inter-Service. How we grew from the 2 Typexes in Mombasa!!

I had occasion to go into the Radio Room sometimes if something wasn't clear on a signal, and on one occasion on night watch the Leading Tel put his finger to his lips. Most of the Tels were locked on to one Jap, which could be boring if that gentleman was not transmitting, while just a few had roving status. After a few minutes he said he had seen one of the Japs come up on a sleeping Wren and knew she would take the signal down in her sleep and wake naturally, but if awakened by my speaking she would lose it. I still have an old blank WT sheet from Anderson".

"A huge amount of the work was on Burma. One night a Commander came into our room and asked me how our traffic was. I said it was very heavy but we just about had our heads above water". "Try and get your tits out dear" he said, "the Army is in a jam in Burma and we are going to send up a lot of spurious radio traffic to make them think an invasion is about to take place and draw them off the Army. This will get them excited". What price inappropriate words and actions in those days? I'm afraid we both just laughed.

We were keenly interested in the intercepted signals which spoke of the movements of Prisoners of War. One of our girls had a husband on the Burma/Thailand railway, another a brother somewhere and I had a cousin in Changi. We always said amongst ourselves that every watch completed was a watch nearer their release. We were all of us, always, totally dedicated to what we did".

Daphne believes the final number of Wrens at Anderson totalled 2000 but one tended to know only the watch-keepers who relieved one and those one worked with.

CONCLUSION

From all the letters and memories I have received from the ex-Wrens who worked in Bletchley Park and its outstations there are none who regretted their time spent in the service.

In spite of strict discipline, many discomforts, frustration in the secrecy of their work and sometimes danger, all felt they had gained from the experience. It had brought out strength of character many were unaware they possessed, and turned naive young girls into confident young women.

Other benefits were the opportunity to meet people from many other social groups from all parts of Britain and overseas, the comradeship and the lasting friendships that were made. For those who went overseas, their horizons were stretched, giving them vistas of exciting new lands, people and cultures, which for many of us encouraged further explorations abroad when peace returned to the world.

Although we had to wait so many years for our work to be recognised by the vast majority of people, we are grateful to know that all we did was worth while and played a part in helping to end hostilities that much sooner.

I have had two personal experiences of appreciation of the work done by those at Bletchley Park. One took place in a restaurant where we were dining with friends from USA. They had been asking me about my time in Bletchley Park and a man dining at the next table had overheard. He tapped me on the shoulder and said, "Did I hear you say you were at Bletchley Park during the war?" I replied, "That's right". He went on, "I was four years at sea during the war, and I just want to say "Thank you" for all you did there".

I was surprised and grateful that he had thought to remember and speak his thanks.

The second occasion was when after an article about me and my book GROWING PAINS – A Teenager's War, was published I received a letter from another wartime sailor, and ex-Convoy Signalman, who wrote from St. Albans and "who served with the Royal Navy from 1942 onwards in the Atlantic and Arctic Oceans and witnessed the awful loss of life". He continued, "You people, possibly saved my life and hundreds of my shipmates. God Bless".

I am sure all those who worked at Bletchley Park will be glad to know that their work was appreciated, even though we had to wait so many years to discover that fact.

We in turn have so much to thank the Merchant and Royal Navy for the sterling work they did in bringing supplies of food and materials to these islands to enable us to keep fighting during those dreadful days when the U-boats were so active.

There are still people who know little about the part Bletchley Park played in World War II. I still have requests to give talks on the subject and have just returned from my third visit to USA to give more talks there. This time a man who was in the German Army came to speak to me after my talk. He said he had known nothing about all this, it was all new to him and he was most impressed.

For those who would like to know more, I would suggest a visit to the Museum run by the Bletchley Park Trust at Bletchley Park, near Milton Keynes, which is open every weekend, would be well worth while.

Gwendoline Page

Bletchley Park Trust is a charity which now owns Bletchley Park and is working to preserve the past and develop the future. If you would like to know more about the exciting work of the Trust, send a donation towards its work, or find out how you can help by leaving a legacy, you should contact: Chris Smith, Finance Director, Bletchley Park Trust, The Mansion, Bletchley, MK3 6EB. Tel: 01908 631120 Email: casmith@bletchleypark.org.uk.